Library
St. Marys Middle School
979 South St. Marys Rd.
St. Marys, PA 15857

ACOLYTES

ALSO BY NIKKI GIOVANNI

POETRY

Black Feeling Black Talk / Black Judgement
Re: Creation
My House
The Women and the Men
Cotton Candy on a Rainy Day
Those Who Ride the Night Winds
The Selected Poems of Nikki Giovanni
Love Poems
Blues: For All the Changes
Quilting the Black-Eyed Pea: Poems and Not Quite Poems
The Collected Poetry of Nikki Giovanni

PROSE

*Gemini: An Extended Autobiographical Statement on My First
     Twenty-five Years of Being a Black Poet*
A Dialogue: James Baldwin and Nikki Giovanni
*A Poetic Equation: Conversations Between Nikki Giovanni and
     Margaret Walker*
Sacred Cows . . . and Other Edibles
Racism 101

EDITED BY NIKKI GIOVANNI

Night Comes Softly: An Anthology of Black Female Voices
Appalachian Elders: A Warm Hearth Sampler
*Grand Mothers: Poems, Reminiscences, and Short Stories About the
     Keepers of Our Traditions*
*Grand Fathers: Reminiscences, Poems, Recipes, and Photos of the
     Keepers of Our Traditions*
*Shimmy Shimmy Shimmy Like My Sister Kate: Looking at the
     Harlem Renaissance through Poems*

FOR CHILDREN

Spin a Soft Black Song
Vacation Time: Poems for Children
Knoxville, Tennessee
The Genie in the Jar
The Sun Is So Quiet
Ego-Tripping and Other Poems for Young People
Rosa

WILLIAM MORROW *An Imprint of* HarperCollins *Publishers*

ACOLYTES
NIKKI GIOVANNI

Library
St. Marys Middle School
979 South St. Marys Rd.
St. Marys, PA 15857

THE FOLLOWING POEMS HAVE BEEN PRINTED ELSEWHERE:

"The Old Ladies Give a Party"

"The Most Wonderful Soup in the World" appeared in *The Great New American Writers Cookbook* © 2003, edited by Dean Faulkner Wells, published by University Press of Mississippi.

"A Poem for My Librarian, Mrs. Long" was published in *Knowledge Quest*.

"Saturday Days"

"The Best Ever Midnight Snack"

"Haiku"

"Doors and Keys"

"Diamonds in the Rough" appeared as the foreword to *Rough Diamonds* © 2003 by Tommy Reamon with Ron Whitenack, published by Triumph Books.

"Harlem Stomp" appeared as the foreword to *Harlem Stomp* © 2004 by Laban Carrick Hill, published by Megan Tingley.

"Don't Hold Me Back" appeared in *Don't Hold Me Back: My Life and Art* © 2003 by Winfred Rembert, published by Cricket Books.

"When Rainbows Laugh"

"Sing Me Home" was published in *Domain*.

ACOLYTES. Copyright © 2007 by Nikki Giovanni. All rights reserved. Printed in the United States of America. No part of this book may be used or reproduced in any manner whatsoever without written permission except in the case of brief quotations embodied in critical articles and reviews. For information address HarperCollins Publishers, 10 East 53rd Street, New York, NY 10022.

HarperCollins books may be purchased for educational, business, or sales promotional use. For information please write: Special Markets Department, HarperCollins Publishers, 10 East 53rd Street, New York, NY 10022.

FIRST EDITION

BOOK DESIGN BY SHUBHANI SARKAR

Library of Congress Cataloging-in-Publication Data

Giovanni, Nikki.
    Acolytes / Nikki Giovanni. — 1st ed.
        p. cm.
    ISBN: 978-0-06-123131-5
    ISBN-10: 0-06-123131-2
        I. Title.

PS3557.I55A63 2007
811'.54—dc22   2006049514

09 10 11 ❖/RRD 10 9 8 7 6 5 4 3 2

THERE IS A SPECIAL NEIGHBORHOOD FOR VERY SPECIAL PEOPLE. It lies deep within the roots of the chestnut tree twining and winding along a spice field. Nutmeg, cinnamon, rosemary, thyme, garlic, giant cloves. White clouds for chairs, blue skies for comfort. Quilts hang from branches if there should be an unanticipated breeze; little lakes of soup just there for the tasting. Unexpectedly the fairies come, rising from their beds of moss, to make caramel cake and fry chicken. It is said they will play Bridge, too, but they always win so it's not quite as much fun. Scott has seen it. Ginney, too. But they came back. Mommy (24 June 2005); Rosa (24 October 2005); and Edna (13 February 2006) decided to stay.

CONTENTS

HOW YOU GONNA SAVE 'EM? 1ST STANZA

It's hard to save 'em
If they won't learn how to pray
Give 'em the blues
And make 'em weep all day

WE GATHER

We are gathered to fulfill a covenant . . . a vow made in cadence to the tramping feet carrying the weary . . . scarred . . . branded bodies harvested for the unspeakably vicious trade in slave labor

We are gathered because a sacred vow was made as these people . . . chained head to toe head to toe head to toe . . . with no room to turn . . . no privacy of body or soul . . . bereft of the comfort their Gods and languages could bring . . . allowed a curiosity . . . a wonder . . . a sense of newness . . . to give them the courage . . . to survive . . . to thrive . . . to find a new world

We are gathered in awe of the people who stood on the auction block . . . bent under the master or the lash . . . clearing land they could not claim . . . growing crops they could not share . . . birthing children they could only love in memory . . . being shamed by powerlessness

We recognize it was never their shame

We gather in celebration of those who utilized the Underground Railroad . . . those who rode it and those who helped others get onboard

We flow bitter tears for those whose freedom was found at the end of a rope

We come to this moment having achieved neither restoration nor reparation but we come . . . we gather together with friends of freedom to commemorate the courageous men and women who have sacrificed their all for the uplifting of humankind . . . we find in this moment the same moon reflecting the same brilliant sun . . . the same stars dancing among the same night skies

We gather because three hundred and eighty-four years ago the "Cargo" that stepped off a Dutch Man-of-War . . . being exchanged for food and water . . . recognizing this was not a good situation which would get better anytime soon . . . still decided to live . . . and fight their battle with a glorious song . . . raised to a new God . . . in a strange land

We gather because it is the right thing to do . . . and it is to that . . . that we say . . . Amen

It's like a bad dream . . . you were in your village with family
and friends when these people came and killed and burned
and stole everything including you

It's like you can't wake up . . . except you hear this whip
this whip this whip and sometimes it hits you and you cry out
and sometimes it hits someone else and you cry out and finally
you realize no matter who it hits it's you who is being hit and
you cry out

But no one answers back

You are rocking you are rocking but not like nana rocked
you with the smell of coconut oil and the smell of soap and the
smell of the stew on the fire and the smell of home it's like a
bad rocking that makes you sick and makes you scared and you
can't find a sound you know and no one knows your sound

It's like the worst dream . . . and people are pulling at
you and pawing at you and it's like a nightmare because it's so
ugly and whatever it is it cannot be about you because if it is
about you then something is wrong with you and nothing can
be wrong with you because if something is wrong with you
then how will you get something right

It's like a lie . . . a huge lie a big white lie that lies
about everything it's a lie about freedom it's a lie about
choices it's a lie about what God said and it sure is a lie who
He said it to cause God did say Make A Joyful Noise and
it's really hard to think you can only make a joyful noise
when things go good cause that's just too easy and what-
ever else God is and whatever else God may be God has
never been easy so Making A Joyful Noise is a Great Thing and
Great Things can only come from Great People

So

Every time any voice is lifted in song the Spirit Rises
and the rising spirit carries the halt and the lame carries the
hurt and the helpless carries the scared and the downtrodden
teaches everyone to raise your spirit by raising your voice so

what we have here in this experience of America is a group of people who would not be downtrodden because they had a song to sing and we have a song to sing and there will be a new song for a new day but every day that there is a song we will sing it and our spirits will rise

A PRAYER FOR NINA

Nina Simone:
Was a beacon against the stormy sea of bigotry and hatred
Was a quilt against the cold of indifference
Was courage to the cowardly
Was boldness to the timid
Was love to the lonely
Was Home to the lost
Is ours for now
And evermore
Amen

HOWL (FOR NINA SIMONE)

(FOREVER YOUNG, GIFTED, AND BLACK)

Howl, Baby
Pull the moon
Down and squeeze
'til there's no
More pain

Tomorrow is coming

Take them to church on Friday nights . . . make them hear the
words and bow down

Make them beg for forgiveness

Tell the truth, my good sister
Don't stop just because it hurts
Tell the truth and let the cooling waters
Let the tears
Fall down
Let us cleanse our evil souls
With the West Wind

Call them out, Girl
Tell them they have to sing with you
Have to sing with Lorraine
Have to sing with Langston
Have to sing for Schwerner, Chaney, and Goodman
Sure the feds will try to trap you
Sure the feds will run you out of the country
Yes J. Edgar Hoover will try to ruin your career
With the same lies he told on King

But you weren't singing
You weren't playing
You weren't giving a damn
For the gramophones
They offered

You were singing
      For a higher power
      To a higher power
      Needing a higher power
To sing you home

You are forever Young
Gifted and Black
You are forever with the righteous
You are forever Nina

Howl, Baby
Call down the sun
To scorch the lies
Call down the stars to write the truth
Call down Call down Call down
And we will worship
At the altar

SING ME HOME
(FOR·LEO SACKS RESPONDING TO KATRINA)

Sing me Home
Wind

Blow a long Blues
Note Knock

Those levies down

Bring on the healing
Waters

Sing through this
Jacket I'm warmed

By your voice

Sing to me,
And I'll come

I'll come home
To the Delta mud
Stepping over

The dead bodies
The floating dogs
The refrigerators

And

The old people
Still connected
To their oxygen

Wind Oh Careless Careless Wind

Sing a north song on
Southbound trains

Sing this fear in
My heart

Take it down my legs
To my toes

Sing Between

And I will laugh

I will bathe
In your waters

I will be satisfied
And Safe

Sing Me Home
Bitch

I need to shine my shoes

THE ROSA PARKS

(A SONG IN RHYTHM)

do the rosa parks
say no no

do the rosa parks
throw your hand in the air

do the rosa parks
say . . . no no

do the rosa parks
tell them: that ain't fair

somebody's lying
rosa parks him
somebody's crying
rosa parks her

shame the bad
comfort the good
do the rosa parks
just like she would

sit down (1-2-3-4-5-6)
stand up (1-2-3-4-5-6)
sit down (1-2-3-4-5-6)
do the rosa parks all over town

THE SEAMSTRESS OF MONTGOMERY

ROSA PARKS

(4 FEBRUARY 1913–24 OCTOBER 2005)

The saddest thing about your death
Is that you missed your funeral

You didn't get to see all the people
Who despised everything you stood for
Have to bend one knee to you
having killed no one
having no weapon other than truth
having made no vows other than to your God
To say "Well done"

History may well show you
Did not need Martin Luther King Jr so much
As he needed you

Only 29 others occupied the place where the nation
Mourns
Military men, political men, police men
And you the seamstress of Montgomery

You were the spark
The flame
The answer

When you sat down
When you kept your seat
When you calmly gave permission
For your arrest
You opened a window
That had been closed an Eternity ago
By a kiss

When you called upon
That quiet strength
When you leaned on
Those Everlasting Arms
The world creaked to a stop
for a brief moment while you inhaled
while you caught your breath
And blew it on the spine of our people

And we would stand up by sitting down
And we would sit down to stand up
And we would kneel in
And pray in
And teach in
And sing in
And vote in
A new day

Thank you, Rosa Parks

Rest Well Mother Parks
Rest Well in the Bosom
Of Abraham

It must have been the waiting. The waiting had to be the worst of it. The only possible, the only possible, the very only possible thing worse than the waiting might be couldn't be would be the waiting being over. The knowing. The knowing they had killed your boy. Not killed. Killed could be an automobile accident. He could be walking down the road with that sort of doo-wop walk he developed as a result of being a breech birth with a knee caught against his chest almost choking him to death before he had a chance to live or that limp could be a result of polio. You had to be grateful that the only scar left was that limp and, of course, that stutter. That stutter that was so frustrating to him because he didn't want to stutter, the other kids would tease him; he wanted to talk strong and manly like he imagined his Daddy did. He wanted to be strong and take care of his mother. And be wonderful and great and show the world how wonderful he was. Yes. Maybe he was walking down the road on the way back to Uncle Mose's house. Dreaming as he was prone to do. Not just daydreaming like some children sitting in a window on a rainy day wanting to go out but dreamy like he had plans like he was talking to someone from somewhere else. Just not paying attention. How many times had you tried to teach him: Pay attention, Bo. And he smiled that babyish smile, that sweet smile, that I'm a good boy Mama smile and said "okay" and went right on not paying attention. Not killed. This was, after all, Mississippi. Killed could be, most likely was, probably was two or three or four mean white boys riding around in a pickup truck. Emmett was on the road alone maybe going to Bryant's to get some bubble gum or some nickel candy maybe some of those windmill cookies 2 for 5 cents and those poor Mississippi crackers were jealous of his shoes and his pants and his white shirt that he wore like he saw a picture of his Daddy wearing a white shirt with the sleeves rolled up. He had the ring on LT May 25, 1943. His Daddy's ring. He was almost big enough to wear it on his ring finger. It

13

was just a little too big so he had wrapped it. Those jealous Mississippi crackers, four or five, maybe six boys riding around in a pickup truck looking for something to do to any girl they could find alone or somebody Black too small to defend himself. Maybe those jealous crazy Mississippi boys grabbed him and wrestled him down. Maybe they hit him and kicked him and threw him in the river. They didn't know they didn't care that he couldn't swim and maybe they watched him flailing and they laughed and drove off and my baby tried and tried but the water pulled him down and he had to give up his spirit. Maybe that's what they mean when they say killed. Emmett was missing. That's what the phone call in the middle of the night said. That he was missing. Mose put his wife on the Chicago train then went calling on everyone who might could help. They didn't want to call me or Mama too early maybe it could get solved without having to make that call. But they had to call. Emmett is missing. Mr. Bryant and Mr. Milam came to get him in the middle of the night. It was 2:00 A.M. and that's not an hour people come to get you when they only intend to teach you a lesson; that's the hour they come when they intend to murder you. There was someone else in the truck. A woman. There was a Black man in the truck bed. "It's Mr. Bryant, Uncle Mose. Open the door." No shame. No sense that there was anything to hide. "I want the boy from Chicago. The one who did all that talking." They offered to pay. They offered to whip him good. They said he was simpleminded and didn't know what he was saying. They said please. But they took my boy. "You don't need no socks, boy. Get on out here." "I never put on shoes without socks," he said. Never understanding the danger. Just a fourteen-year-old boy trying to impress his Mississippi cousins. They would laugh at his stutter; they would ape his doo-wop walk. He wanted to show them he wasn't afraid. Talk to that woman in the store, if you're so tough. She's a white woman. If you so tough in Chicago, talk to that woman. They knew. They knew the danger. They knew he would probably take a good whipping from somebody: Mr. Bryant, Uncle Mose. Somebody would show him that just because he was from Chicago his Mama was from Webb and they were from Money and this is Mississippi and the cousins knew how this system worked not the cripple stuttering boy from Chicago. With his ring and his pants and his soft shoes and his white shirt. And that hat on the side of his head. They would show him. Never thinking three days later there would be a knock at the door. At first nobody knew. Whatever was said was said. The Black community held its breath but Bryant was away taking fish or crabs or something with his half brother J. W. Milam. Milam was a mean cracker. Bragged he knew how to take care of niggers. Didn't hesitate to show anyone. Three days passed and nothing was said. But Bryant came home. Tired. Unhappy. With not much more money than he left with. Working too hard for a good-looking white man and not making much money. Some little Black Judas whispered: What you going to do about that boy from Chicago who did all that talking to your wife? Carolyn Bryant hadn't said a word about it. She knew what would happen. She didn't have to be a nice person, a concerned person, a person with a conscience. She just knew what would happen and she didn't want it on her plate. Milam's wife who stayed with Carolyn while the men were away trying to make a little extra money knew what would happen. She knew what her husband would do. She knew what he did to her; she knew what he did to the children. She didn't want it on her plate. But some little Black Judas without even the thirty pieces without even a piece of candy or a cookie. Some little jealous Black Judas whispered to Bryant: What you going to do? Did he think there would be a show? That Bryant would take Emmett to the front of the store, strip his shirt off and give him five or ten lashes? Did he think it would be fun to see my boy, a fourteen-year-old, a barely fourteen-year-old, cry for mercy? Did he think that would make his life in Mississippi any better? What could he have been thinking? But whatever he was thinking it couldn't have been that Bryant and Milam would take Emmett out at 2:00 A.M. throw him in the back of the pickup and take him to Milam's barn. No one would think they would strip his clothes off of him to make fun of his penis. No one would think they would handle him like they did. That they would beat him and beat him and then the cutting started. Then they beat him and Emmett's eye popped out. There was blood, Emmett's blood all over that barn. The Black man beat him, too. Just so the white men could think he would not testify against them. Finally, mercifully, they put a bullet in his head. But I know my baby was gone way before that. I know Jesus reached into that barn and took Emmett away. I know they sat on a cloud and watched the horror but Emmett was not in that barn when they started putting things in every orifice that they could. Emmett was not in that barn when they started the cutting. No. Emmett was not in that barn. They wrapped the barbed wire around what was left of his neck and told that Negro to attach it to the cotton-gin fan. They hauled his body to the Tallahatchie River. Even they must have known what a horrible thing they had done. Even they must have been ashamed. But, no, killed did not describe what they did to my boy. Three days later when his body was found they wanted to bury him in Mississippi. I wanted him home in Chicago. I wanted the world to see what they did to my boy. I wanted Emmett's death to be the last death. I wanted Emmett's death to kill American innocence. I wanted Emmett's death to be not only the death of my boy but *the death of innocence*. I wanted Mississippi, I wanted America, to give us justice. And I prayed that I would live long enough to see it.

WE GO ON

(FOR NANNIE HAIRSTON)

We go on

Because there is this history uncelebrated . . .
unacknowledged . . .
unwanted . . .
That takes place each Sunday
        in church
Each Saturday
        at the juke joint
And every day of the week
When we try to make a house
A home

No one wants to understand
The faith it takes to be
A mother
A grandmother
A pillar of a distressed community

No one wants to understand
The courage it takes to be
A deacon
A janitor
A miner in the crumbling mines

Yet neither our fate
Nor our faith
Can reside in the hands
Of those who don't care
Of those who let greed be their God
Of those who tear down our meeting halls
Burn down our churches
Laugh at our steadfastness
And say "Oh, I'm sorry"
When caught in the web of lies

We go on answering
        a trumpet call
Following
        the living savior
Hoping
        for a better tomorrow

We go on because of
The strength of our soldiers
The righteousness of our battle
The need of the saved to prevail over the damned

We go on

Because we have good men and women
Good boys and girls
Good people
Who want this history
Others would destroy
To live

There must have been a silence. Not a moan, not a mumbling word. But a silence. The shock. The absolute disbelief. The incredible stunning astonishing gaping shame. At capture. The incomprehensible knowledge that the sun stood still. The stars extinguished their twinkles. The winds and the rains fled underground. The moon withdrew its comforting glow. Not only the silence of different languages. Different images. Different words for the same objects. The holocaustic silence of the unthinkable now made manifest. The captured did not understand their captors. Nor each other. They only understood the chains. The whips. The desecrations. The destructions. The horror. Yet that should not. Could not. Have been the reason for silence.

Maybe there was nothing more to say.

The long lines on the trips to the coast. The babies crying. Then being thrown into the bush. Or run through with a bayonet. The mothers screaming. And fighting back. And being murdered also. The animals that lived the trail of the slavers. Grew used to everything coming easy. Grew expectant. And fat. And lazy. Grew more evil. In their own imaginations. Grew impossible to live with. Themselves. Anyone else. Grew crazy in the trade. Of human flesh. And human souls. Prayed at the river. Tithed to the church. Searched their Bible. And still went in the night to the captured. And still sought relief and understanding. And still tried to justify.

Someone had to look. To remember.

The screaming commands. The cracking whips. The kicking boots indicating time: To go to the big ships. To be brave and strong. To find a way to stay human. Some will jump. And some will expire. Some will kill their captors. And some will escape. But most will find themselves. On an auction block. Being intruded upon. Being violated. Being branded and corralled. But the spirit stayed. And the heart remembered. They were silent because there were no words to express it.

The salt of the tears. The salt of the blood. The salt in the wounds. All knew.

It cannot be unusual. That the slaves left no written records. They were denied rudimentary materials. But they sang a song. And they preached a service. And their story was codified. And sanctified. And passed along. And the second voice of the people ripped from Africa. Whipped into the New World. Molded on the plantations. Came from their feet. The feet spoke clearly when they ran away. And they ran away. And away. And away so much that the South had to make America safe for slavery by passing The Fugitive Slave Law which would not have been needed. If the slaves had not spoken so loudly. Through Gabriel Prosser. Through Denmark Vesey. Through Nat Turner. Through the Underground Railroad. They spoke so loudly. A man named John Brown. Who wanted his sons. To be free men. Heard them. Prayed about it. Took his sons. And led the charge. Against Harpers Ferry. Against the corrupt federal government. Against his own white skin. And started the war. That freed the slaves. That offered to free America. If America hadn't been too venal. Too stupid. Too arrogant. To understand what a gift had been offered.

It is not unusual that so few found a way. It is unusual that so many did.

And out of the hearts. And hopes. Out of the souls and salvation. The words tumbled. The words ran to the riverside. Shouted from the mountains. Wove themselves into blankets. Wrapped themselves in Gelees. Whispered in the night. A freedom song. A brave and wondrous story not of survival but of triumph. Through thunder and fire. Through gentle rain. Through heavy, violent winds. Through magnolia breezes. The Americans who were once captured and enslaved. The Americans who were once considered a little less than chattel. The Americans who didn't want to come and were not happy to be here. Now became not the voice of the slaves. But the voice of America. It is not nearly so unusual that the printed word is spoken. But that the spoken word is printed. Stamped. Paginated. Made available. To the world. To tell the story. Of a person. Of a people. Of the undeniable will. To prevail.

So we come to these voices. To Zora Neale Hurston. To Langston Hughes. To Richard Wright. To Gwendolyn Brooks. To Lorraine Hansberry. To all of us who are . . . in the mighty words of Martin Luther King, Jr. *Free At Last! Free At Last!* Free to break our Silence. Free to tell our story. Free to love and laugh.

What fascinates me are the skills; I am in awe of the courage. How did those slaves, those who were in chattel slavery; those who were constantly being told they were no more than a mule and a lot less than a good horse; those who were given the leftovers to eat and the throwaways to wear: what made them know they were human? It is current to laugh at the language skills of our ancestors and the lack of language skills of young-sters today but those who came before like those who are now with us have this burning desire to follow the Drinking Gourd. No one taught astronomy to the slaves. No one asked them out in the clarity of night to point to the Pleiades, to marvel at Venus rising tucked against the new moon. There were no schools for moss and there were no trails since trails meant people and people meant capture. Yet they followed that star and cut a new trail and gave the world another meaning of freedom. How proud we all must be of these efforts. We know many were captured and suffered unspeakable pain but many many more found the new land. And today we on Earth are watching our probe explore Saturn; we are poised to consider the first human beings going to Mars. We will once again find humankind in an unknown space with an unsure welcome. The more we understand those captured souls who endured Middle Passage, who ran from the plantations and who yet sang a grateful song to their God, the better we prepare our-selves for life beyond the known. I am so honored to be a part of the National Underground Railroad Freedom Center. The past is our future.

There must be a certain irony that a people who had migrated across a big and unforgiving ocean for religious freedom as well as the opportunity to have a more prosperous life took upon themselves the burden of enslaving and the hypocrisy that slaves were less than people with no desire to know God nor celebrate the freedoms and responsibilities such knowledge brings.

For several generations slaves were denied formal acknowledgment of The Word other than, perhaps, a few house slaves who accompanied their masters to church to attend to any needs that might have arisen. The slaves in the field didn't care what the big house did: They knew there had to be a God and they knew they had to be able to both thank Him for life and petition Him for deliverance.

As the slave rebellions became more numerous, culminating in Denmark Vesey's great challenge to that system, slaves were forbidden to gather together without a white man present. The regular Sunday worship was attended by the captured with the thankfulness that a day of rest will bring. They came together Sunday mornings to hear The Word and praise the Lord in a manner that suited those who oversaw. But the hunger to express a thankfulness and a need would not be satisfied by being on exhibit to those who watched.

The slaves drifted away from the secure places to find a hideaway to worship as they saw fit. They created and sang songs; they maintained the rituals they recalled from their African past. They also carried messages. The Hush Harbors were sanctuaries but had they been caught, and when they were caught, punishment was brutal and swift. Anything from whipping to being sold away from family and friends to lynching or burning to death could be expected. Yet they continued to seek privacy, solace, and peace. One can almost hear them ask: "Shall we gather at the river? The beautiful, beautiful river?" No matter what price they might have to pay, gather they did. And both preserved and created a culture.

One of the most exciting periods in American history, if not the history of the world, is the Harlem Renaissance. A people who were chattel only a generation earlier took over the cultural quilt of America and warmed the world.

Coming out of the reactionary Black Laws created to undo the progressive 13th, 14th, and 15th Amendments to the Constitution, the Black population started voting with its feet and walking away from the brutality and hardships of the South. They came to St. Louis, Chicago, and ultimately to Harlem seeking peace, prosperity, and freedom.

It is an amazing piece of propaganda that Black people were lazy. Aside from the obvious impossibility that a slave could be lazy and also alive, Blacks have worked, and worked hard and successfully, in every field of endeavor they have been allowed to pursue. A people who were lynched, bombed, and burned out by a white population for exercising citizenship rights, then had to watch those same terrorists claim Blacks were not able and did not want to vote, go to school, or participate in the life of the community and country were aghast at the blaspheme. The dirty work of the aristocratic class was done by dumb, ignorant, prejudiced, hateful, illiterate white folks who had only their skin color to justify their breathing air, drinking water, and eating food. What a crazy irony that the people who had faithfully cleared the forest and planted the crops that would be staples of the young country, who had valiantly fought each war, who had remained good and faithful friends through natural and man-made disasters were now subject to unspeakable crimes. Blacks had had enough. They left for the cities. They left for their physical and emotional well-being. They left to give their children a better chance.

There can be no doubt that they were scared. They had nothing but their great hearts, which had carried them through two hundred of the darkest years of Euro-American history. How these years came to be years of shame for Black people is beyond understanding. It is not we who kidnapped, raped, and ravished a people. It is not we who carried diseased blankets to a defeated foe. It is not we who continue to struggle against equality and opportunity for everyone.

The Harlem Renaissance brought together a gaggle of Blacks who sang their plantation songs then made a variation to call it *blues* then made a variation to call it *jazz*. The *Spirituals* and *jazz* are now considered the American music but that can only be so if Blacks are an American people.

The Renaissance can also be viewed through the literature. It was a great literature that was nurtured and created. Countee Cullen remembered a visit to Baltimore, Claude McKay demanded *if we must die let it not be like hogs*, Jesse Fauset said *There Is Confusion*, Zora Neale Hurston laughed at everybody, and the incomparable Langston Hughes wanted ultimately to know *What Happens To A Dream Deferred*, especially after his beautiful and eloquent *I've Known Rivers*, among others, found the voice of justice, found the voice of hope, remembered to voice a prayer and put it in a book that others would hear, identify with, and understand the story. The visual artists had to overcome the mean images that had been perpetuated during slavery and Reconstruction. Movies like *Birth of a Nation* and *Gone With the Wind* had to be countered with true images of a people struggling to find a place for themselves in a nation ashamed of its past. **Harlem Stomp** looks at these brave and wonderful people. **Harlem Stomp** finds both truth and joy in the struggle to rebirth. **Harlem Stomp** is an American history of an American people redefining this great American nation.

Of the many foundations upon which humans rest, words are probably the most solid. I remember the old children's song: "Sticks and stones may break my bones but words will never touch me." Which is totally not true. We remember cruel things people have said long after we have forgotten the person. We remember the little hurts of not being invited to a birthday party or even worse the whisper that we won't get a date for the prom. We remember the teacher who said we were dumb and we remember the prejudiced epithets that Countee Cullen spoke so beautifully against. But words without heart, without emotion, without passion are themselves less meaningful. Words need to combine with words to make not a better word but a more meaningful metaphor. Poetry. When arrogance calls it should always be poetry that answers thereby granting a stay to humankind's feelings of omnipotence. When love calls it must be poetry that answers bringing the sweet perfume of gentleness as our hearts pound and pound; when courage calls it will always be poetry that answers as we rise above ourselves to bring about a better thing. When war calls, poetry is the only answer. Poetry says No to destruction and Yes to possibility. Poetry is a good idea. A good friend. A good neighbor. Let's write poems.

Saturdays Mommy, Gary, and I dusted the entire house then walked to the grocery store then put everything away then sat at the table (which was neither dining room nor kitchen just a yellow table in between) and had lunch. We always played "What I Am Eating" and I always had "roast tom turkey" which I must have thought sounded terribly elegant and sophisticated. Usually there was a tearjerker on television and we would watch Joan Crawford or Bette Davis or Lana Turner and cry and cry and cry. In Cincinnati at my parents' home I always liked Saturday days but Saturday nights Daddy would holler at Mommy autumn, winter, and spring. I couldn't wait for summer because we went to Knoxville to visit our grandparents.

Directly across from 400 Mulvaney there was Cal Johnson Park. It should have been Dr. Cal Johnson Park because Dr. Johnson, a black man, had purchased this land and willed it to the city for the use of black children in perpetuity. It stands yet. There was a creek in the back where our tennis balls would be forever lost and if you cut through the park you could reach Vine Street in half the time without having to climb the Mulvaney Street hill. Grandmother and I saw the Silas Green Revue there which had to be one of their last shows. In this age of segregation the swimming pool for black kids was in Mechanicsville but we at CJP had the swings.

One of the least known aspects of my personality is that I am dutiful. Anything I have to do I do and do as cheerfully as I can. But I have to admit I actually like housekeeping. There is something about order that brings peace and comfort. On Knoxville Saturdays Grandpapa would go to the market. This is most likely because Grandmother was both very pretty and very mouthy. She took no prisoners. Grandpapa already knew not to let Louvenia near anyone or anything that would upset her. If, for example, Grandmother had gone to the market, one of the white guys would probably say something totally out of line. Grandmother would verbally abuse him then come home and tell Grandpapa. Grandpapa would be honor bound to go back up to the Gay Street Market and ask for an apology. Most likely that would not be forthcoming so Grandpapa would be forced to shoot the man. The word would spread in both communities that John Brown Watson had shot Mr. White So and So and the black community would hunker down while the white community would liquor up and come dark the whites would swarm down on Mulvaney Street baying for the blood of Grandpapa who would be lynched, the house burned down and all sorts of various sadness would be visited upon black Knoxville before the Tennessee militia was called out to enforce the peace. The great thing about my Grandpapa is not only that he was smart but that he could see the logical end to most endeavors so Grandpapa went to the market and Grandmother and I stayed home to clean.

I'm still not sure what it is about living rooms that makes black women crazy. Every Saturday you dust and dust that room wiping the plastic covering the furniture and since we did not have a vacuum cleaner running the mechanical broom over the carpet. Grandmother didn't change the beds until Monday but we brought out the Old English polish for the furniture and the silver polish for the teaset and I always liked the Bruce's wax in a can for the floors. It's not, by the way, that I like mice because I don't have any particular affection for mice but since we lived in a small town there was always the chance a mouse would get in so Grandmother kept a trap set. I still don't think anything should be in a trap so I hit on the idea of waxing the pantry floor. I was thinking if the mice smelled the wax they would know someone lived there and go on. I don't know what the mice thought but in all my years of living with my Grandparents we only caught one mouse. . . . and I liked to think he was already sick. I not only like housekeeping but I am quick. I put my head down and got it done. Grandmother would always go behind you to make sure it had been done right but what she never knew is that I can't stand to be corrected so I always do my very best to get whatever it is right. I did. So I got to go swinging.

I've always thought swinging should be an Olympic sport. I knew, in fact, when synchronized swimming became a "sport" Double Dutch would be next. I admire Double Dutch. Those ropes would pop and the girls would turn faster and faster and the girls running in and jumping out would dance a dance that would make ballet dancers weep from envy. They would jump up and twirl and pass each other and one foot then flip to their hands then flip back up and I would stand amazed. I have no sense of rhythm. All my rhythm is in my head. But I could swing. Swinging took courage and patience and balance, and the most difficult maneuver is the dismount. I grew up with iron swings that were set in concrete; none of those recycled things for me. The swing was hard black rubber connected to links of iron.

These were swings to take you to the moon. The object, for those who do not swing, was to stand in the seat and pump up. You pumped up as high as you could go. You were actually trying to reach parity with the top bar. When you got "even with the bar" (to which I ascribed 10 points) you "kicked out and sat down in the seat" (10 points). If you missed the seat you could still hold on but it looked really ragged. You then pumped once or twice more to show control (10 points) then (and this was the final crucial ending) you "bailed out." You got 20 points for a perfect landing. If you fell or tumbled over, you lost points accordingly. Sort of like a poor girls' parallel bars. The dismount was everything! And I would practice and practice. Pump and jump; pump and jump. Then Grandmother would call me to lunch. But I was ready. I knew I was ready. I was prepared to go for the gold medal. All I needed was a chance.

QUILTS

(FOR SALLY SELLERS)

Like a fading piece of cloth
I am a failure

No longer do I cover tables filled with food and laughter
My seams are frayed my hems fall-
ing my strength no longer able
To hold the hot and cold

I wish for those first days
When just woven I could keep water
From seeping through
Repelled stains with the tightness of my weave
Dazzled the sunlight with my
Reflection

I grow old though pleased with my memories
The tasks I can no longer complete
Are balanced by the love of the tasks gone past

I offer no apology only
This plea:

When I am frayed and stained and drizzled at the end
Please someone cut a square and put me in a quilt
That I might keep some child warm

And some old person with no one else to talk to
Will hear my whispers

And cuddle
Near

ON A RAINY AUTUMN DAY

On a rainy autumn day
I lay on sheets washed
In 20 Mule Team Borax
Hung to dry
By sun and southern wind
Smoothed
Onto an overstuffed ticking
Mattress
Covered by a single weight
                single stitched
                quilt

My body drinks in
The cooling embrace
And I smile
Dreaming
Of my grandmother's laughter

Old lace handkerchiefs . . . as delicate as a spiderweb
     against the sun
A snuff box made of ivory . . . from a visit to Ghana
The quilt . . . stuffed with rice sacks that great-grandmother
     patched
A spoon time has so blackened the silver will not shine
     through again . . . but sterling it is
That Scofield Bible with the leather almost showing the human
     oils of the hands that held it
And shoes run over . . . at the heels . . . why do we even keep
     them
Her recipe for hush puppies greasy with splatter
If the Parker Brothers pen was put on auction a cruise to the
     Carribbean could be purchased
Photographs with faces but no names . . . friends . . . lovers
     maybe . . . that one is a graduation that one a wedding . . .
     a picnic somewhere . . . everybody laughing
A string of fake pearls . . . real diamond rings in a cracked
     china cup
Evening in Paris beside the face powder and lipstick
White gloves for ushering at Sunday services . . . Black leather
     gloves for more secular concerns
A little Tiffany lamp . . . a handmade comb of wood . . .
     rhinestones in another
Doilies . . . Vicks . . . McGawans Rubbing Lotion . . . Carter's
     Little Liver Pills
A room . . . covered by an old Oriental rug
A bed . . . covered by a white chenille spread
And I . . . looking through the front bedroom window . . .
     recognize I too . . . am old

CRIASKEW'S FAMILY

Families are:

Dusting the living room on Saturday morning
(in case the preacher comes by on Sunday)
Sitting patiently at the beauty parlor to get a curl
Watching grandpapa wring the chicken's neck
(So grandmother can fry it for Sunday after church dinner)
Helping grandmother hull strawberries for the shortcake
Breaking green beans and cutting the ham hock
Mashing the potatoes
Rolling the miniature Parker House rolls
Sitting on the glider as the sun goes down
Being happy that it's summer

And you are home
With your grandparents

PAINT ME LIKE I AM

I know this   it is difficult to grow up
                  it always was
                  it always will be

I know this   nobody can tell you how to do it
                  You just make the same mistakes and
                  You just thrill to the same excitement

I know this   Life is a good idea

I think   it is illogical
                      to assume there is no other life in the
                      Universe
I think   the possibility of re-creating our-
                  selves is in our hands
I think   humans are not the only thinking beings
                  we just happen to be the only species
                  that we respect

It is our loss.

We need   to listen to those who are forming
We need   to hear the cry of those in pain
We need   to respect the fear and embrace the longing
                      of those who are new to the wilderness

I know   imagination is a good idea
I know   those forging forward must embrace
                creativity
I know   humans will shrivel from emotional needs
                   before we die of starvation or dehydration
                The body will take care of itself.

We need food for the Soul

            We need poetry . . . We deserve poetry
We owe it to ourselves to re-create ourselves
              and find a different if not better way to live

Paint Me Hopeful   Paint Me Futuristic   Paint Me Nikki
              I'm A Poet

THE CHANGE OF LIFE

(TO MOMMY 1 JANUARY 1919–24 JUNE 2005)

This is what I remember:
In Kindergarten we made lanterns . . . we cut our paper strips . . . glued them together bowed them out and we had a lantern
I was always neat . . . always very neat . . . I am still neat . . . Someone took my lantern . . . When it was time to take home our projects the only one left had glue everywhere . . . the strips were cut crooked . . . it didn't bow . . . it was not my lantern . . . I was always last . . . I'm still always late . . . late . . . last . . . and not terribly concerned about it . . . I left that lantern and lost a bit of my heart . . . to the classmate who took mine . . . This is so clear to me . . . I never mentioned it to Mommy

      Fall in the 7th Grade . . . the leaves crispy red . . . yellow . . . orange . . . Before class we all stand around . . . a large . . . very large Oak Tree in the center of the driveway . . . all of us trying to be cool . . . Jimmy . . . poor Jimmy with buck-teeth and never the right shoes or shirts or pants . . . trying to fit in . . . to make us like him . . . Me . . . I'm in with the in crowd . . . but Jimmy had buck teeth that were a bit yellow . . . the wrong shoes . . . and a bulge, it seemed, in his pants all the time . . . We laughed . . . at him . . . the Nuns, we knew, just would not allow sex . . . I discovered when I went to the bathroom one morning . . . a way out of gym . . . I told Mommy right away

      I don't remember:
Cramps . . . discomfort . . . accidents . . . liking or disliking . . . tampons or napkins

      I do remember:

Being in awe of the girls who took the pill and knew when "their friend" was late or on time . . . one day mine didn't come . . . but my son did . . . and I went back to not . . . remembering

This is what I think:
I have been blessed with a poor memory . . . I have forgot-
ten crazy night sweats . . . I have forgotten crying, no heav-
ing, when the old lady goes each day to the mailbox and there
is no mail until her neighbor notices and sends her a Hall-
mark . . . I try to forget how lonely she must be . . . I don't
remember waving good-bye to my Grandmother after we
buried Grandpapa . . . her standing on the front porch so small
and all alone . . . and me not understanding why I couldn't
make it better . . . I don't remember my anger at witnessing
the face of Emmett Till . . . nor my fear when Four Little Girls
were murdered one Sunday . . . I think I just shook my head
No when that crazy crazy thing in Colorado accused Kobe . . .
I have forgotten to be afraid of change . . . change is good . . .
change is necessary . . . change is life . . . and life is change
        I wish:
I had been a better friend to my lovers . . . and a better lover
to my friends . . . I wish I had said the good things I thought . . .
instead of the mean ones . . . A change of life gives second
chances . . . and life changes are natural and good . . . Before
he died I said to my father: "It hasn't been that bad . . . I guess
we all do love each other" . . . But Mommy's still here . . . and
I'm more sure . . . and I tell her every day

I am in Mexico. I study sea turtles. I have no idea why. I also like hippopotami. There must be a reason. My sister has lung cancer. Before I left for the baby sea turtles I fired her doctor. He was not, I think, a bad man. He just didn't have an answer. And like a lot of folk who lack answers, he decided there was nothing to be done. I had to hope he was wrong. But right or wrong, he needed to be fired.

I am in my mother's bedroom. She is in a hospital bed which she does not like. She has gotten out of it twice now. Mostly she has not fallen but slipped when sliding through the bed supports. She has total control of her bladder and still can go to the bathroom on her own steam. We worry because she seems so frail. She is terminal. And none of us like that. I fired her first doctor, too. I don't like bad news.

And I was diagnosed with lung cancer ten years ago. I got lucky. I am still here. At least my mother will not have to bury me. Or my sister. Things remain in order.

And this is the culmination of a young woman's thoughts. Youth is a good idea. We are strong and determined. We have a sense of justice. Me, I only wanted to be a voice. Coming as I do from a voiceless people, a people who were denied freedom, a language, an education; coming as I do from a people who had only a song with which to tell our story and a poem with which to dream . . . I wanted to be a voice.

My mother is a sneak reader, she has read all my books but she never discusses them with me. She knows most of my poems by heart. I know this because something will come up, some little thing, some unimportant thing, and she will quote me. She collects my Keys to the Cities, all my Delta Sigma Theta elephants, any photographs with important people. She especially likes the photo with Hillary Clinton. My favorite is with Edna Lewis. Mother makes the best bean soup; Miss Lewis fries the best chicken. I am the best eater. Mommy has never hesitated to say she is proud of me, even when she is not. But the Grammy nomination stands out because she always thought I should have had one. She took me aside to say: "I am so very proud of you." I didn't win but I went to L.A. And I looked good. She was already too sick when Oprah recognized me as one of the Twenty-five Legends.

And so one era ends, my mother and my beginning career. My aunt is crying. She reminds my sister and me that she has never known a time without her oldest sister, our mother. Neither have my sister and I. I am sad today. And I probably will be for a long time. I still miss my grandmother who died thirty-six years ago. My father died twenty-three years ago the day after my birthday. Mommy went into the hospital June 8. I recently turned sixty-two. I am twenty-four years younger than Mommy. That's all I have to say.

I AM MIGHTY MOUSE

(F O R   D O R O T H Y   H E I G H T)

The reason I think I am Mighty Mouse is this:

Once upon a time a long time ago when I was a very young woman and had not at that time actually met Dr. Height she made me know how important it is for women to have confidence in each other.

Marge Schott, your typical bigot, spread her hatred over her ball club, the Cincinnati Reds. She used the *n* word for her players of color ... she also collected Nazi memorabilia ... plus she said "Hitler" as in the holocaust "wasn't a bad man ... he just went a 'little' too far." So that would leave us to think that one million dead Jewish people were not too much but six million were? The bigot had a problem.

This is how she intended to solve it: the National Council of Negro Women was having its annual dinner in Sharonville which is a suburb of Cincinnati. Someone had informed Marge Schott that she should attend that meeting to show she was not a racist. Most people would have rejected the call from the Schott folk and turned down their donation, too, but the need to make money overcame the need to make sense. The head of the Cincinnati chapter of NCNW as it turns out was a friend of my sister's. Mamie Hall was married to Ted Hall who was a good friend of McMurtry, who was a great love of my sister's. Mamie and Gary hung out together because of their mutual interest in Mac and Ted and when Ted and Mamie married and moved in with his folks in Lincoln Heights they were even closer. Gary had married someone else or maybe a couple of folks by the time Marge Schott was becoming the poster girl for bigots but I, ever a fool for family ties, had agreed to return to Cincinnati to give the keynote speech.

This is what happened: a lot of folk were at the dinner because they saw Marge as fresh meat that they could use. Many wanted to save her, most wanted to use her. I wanted to make sense.

Dorothy Height is one of the most astute political minds

of the twentieth century. There are no major decisions made concerning Civil Rights that Dr. Height has not participated in. There . . . you see her on the left hand of Martin Luther King, Jr., at the March On Washington. You don't see her, but she's there under the strong brave and brilliant arm of Mary McLeod Bethune learning the ways of power. You see her at the Big Six meetings. This wonderful President of Delta Sigma Theta who determined that her mentor, Mrs. Bethune, would have a statue on federal land. And she made that happen.

Dottie was worried. She understood the significance of Marge Schott sitting at a table under the banner of NCNW: She knew it would appear as if everything was all right; Schott had simply been misunderstood. That bothered Dottie. She was looking for a way to keep the reputation of the NCNW clean. The keynote speaker would be the key.

What Dorothy Height decided: Dottie said to her aide "I must speak with our keynoter. I must make her or him understand what is at stake. Marge Schott must not be allowed to get away with this. Who is the speaker?" Her aide called Cincinnati to ask who is the keynoter. Nikki Giovanni she was told. The aide reported back to Dr. Height: it is Nikki Giovanni.

"Nikki?" asked Dottie. "Are you sure?" "Yes, Dr. Height, I am sure." "Well then," said the mighty one, "I'm going to bed." "Don't you want to talk with her?" Height was asked. "Oh, no. Nikki will take care of it. Good night."

What it meant: when I heard Dr. Dorothy Height had such faith in me that I would do the right thing I felt so proud I could have burst. I have always admired Dorothy Height and I am so proud to know she had confidence in me. I wanted to step onto that stage and say ". . . here I come to save the day . . ." but I didn't. I did tell Marge Schott she needed to step down. And I did make ESPN for the only time in my life. But mostly I knew the pride that comes from knowing Dorothy Height went to bed. Never worrying that I would carry the day.

TODAY: FOR MARI EVANS

I have made this too hard. I have wanted to be perfect. Love does that to you. We forget we love our friends. We forget we fell in love with our third-grade teacher; fell madly in love with our aunt who was always so sharp, so cool, so run-down men's slippers covering red-painted toenails with a cigarette hanging from her mouth cool. So competent standing in the back door, some Nina Simone moan coming through the window screen apron folded down halfway waiting for something. What. We didn't know. But we wanted very much to grow up and wait too. We forget that love is not just for fried chicken or deviled eggs or men who come and go through our lives. Love is for our friends, too. And we want it to be perfect. Because we are introducing her to others we might love if we knew them and someone we know anyhow we do love because they complete us. They are the readers; we the writers. We reverse that sometimes and sometimes we are both but we always know the person on the other side of the poem is a lover. And we love that, too.

I have made this too hard. I have sweated over it, agonized over it, worried it to death because I wanted it to be perfect. So that the love would come through. There are things, like fudge, that must be taken up at exactly the right time, enough air whipped into them to take the glaze off, poured when still warm and cut before set. Something like a colored girl getting her hair "done" on Saturday afternoon for Sunday Services. Everything must take place in pace and on time. Much like saying "Yes" and sometimes "No." Timing is everything.

This shouldn't be so hard. This is a part of the **Continuum.** And we do go on. Scared. Unsure. Troubled by the dark. Blinded by desire. We do go on. We continue. And because it isn't perfect. Because it is hard. Someone will see that someone tried. And someone will know that someone loves. We come home because we have no other place to go. And that is hard. We continue. Because we don't forget we love our friends. And the soup they simmer. And the photographs they shoot. And the songs they sing. We go on. Because it is the hard thing to do. And we owe ourselves the difficulty.

AFTER THE DROWNING

After the drowning
the calming waters come
closing a whole that never
opened
Why not take the Champagne flute
dip it in the salty cold
water
and drink a toast
to all
that never was

HOW YOU GONNA SAVE 'EM? 2ND STANZA

How you gonna save 'em
If they can't learn how to pray
Give 'em a song I guess
To chase those blues
Away

I'm a native Tennessean. I was born there. During the age of segregation. When you couldn't go to the same amusement park. Or the same movie theater. When the white guys would cruise up and down the streets and call out to you. When the black guys were afraid of being lynched. But we went to church each Sunday. And we sang a precious song. And we found a way not to survive. Anything can survive. But to thrive. And believe. And hope.

I'm a native Tennessean. I was born there. But I was only two months old when my mother and father moved my sister and me to Cincinnati. During the age of segregation. When Dow Drugstore wouldn't serve us. When neighborhoods were redlined. But at least Mommy could get a job teaching. And Daddy could get a job behind a desk. And after all if you are a college graduate that is the least you can expect. Though the Pullman Porters took us South each summer. And watched over us with an unfailing faith. And got us from there and here.

I'm from Knoxville. I was born there. In the only state in rebellion that didn't have to undergo Reconstruction. In the Volunteer State that sent as many for one side as another. In an area where if I just have to have a car break down I would prefer any holler to any city neighborhood. But there was no work. And no way. And the "chronic angers" that flared would chase us to Ohio. We were not Liza crossing the river. Just four people . . . two in love and two who were loved . . . who needed to put to rest the rage.

But the rage stayed. And someone had to go. I chose me. But I was born there. So the going was a coming. I am a native Tennessean.

I take no joy in Davy Crockett. Nor Jim Bowie. They were wrong to be at the Alamo. They were wrong to fight for the theft. I love James Agee. I loved *Thunder Road* though I, a native Tennessean, was not allowed to play a bit part when the crew came to town to film the movie. Ingrid Bergman and

Anthony Quinn came to take a *Walk in the Spring Rain*. And despite it all I like Andrew Jackson. At least he knew the big guys were wrong.

I'm a native Tennessean. I graduated Fisk University in Nashville. I know that the Freedmen paid for that school. Nobody gave them anything. Pennies and nickels and prayer and determination. The Freedmen paid for it. And many others. I know the American Missionary Society took the money the Jubilee Singers made to save Fisk and used it for other purposes. I know the American Missionary Society was wrong. I was educated by the singers of those songs. I love those songs. How could I not love Nashville? How could I not love Dinah Shore who invited the Jubilee Singers to sing at The Grand Ole Opry then had to hear the rumors. She sang on. Sang until she saw the USA in her Chevrolet. Ummmompt! I once saw her on a plane. I was going to the cabin. She was in first class. I said: "Hey." She smiled and said "Hey" back.

When I got Georgia on my mind I rode the Chattanooga Choo-Choo to Lookout Mountain. I saw Memphis and was enchanted. From the mighty Mississippi Gracefully turning all red to Beale Street beats at midnight. All those blues from so many bloods. Decided to turn my blues to Memphis gold. W. C. Handy. Bobby "Blue" Bland. B. B. King. The late great Johnny Ace. Stax and stacks of music. American music. The Athens of the South held Tennessee music. But Memphis put the tears to the lonely. And crossed over. Everybody wants to rock to my rhythm. I am Memphis. I heard the shots that took Martin. I know who killed The King.

I'm a native Tennessean. I know what it is to be free. I am singing the country blues. I am whittling a wooden doll. I am underground mining coal. I am running moonshine. I am a white boy with a banjo. Native to West Africa. I am a black boy with a twang. Native to the hills. I am smart. I am cool. I am unafraid. I am free. Yeah. I am a native Tennessean.

I AM IN THE WATER

I am in the water
I cannot swim
I am brave and unafraid
The waves are not daunting

Once I dreamed
To be a world-class swinger
To take my swing so high
To go even with the bar
And to smoothly dismount
Landing perfectly in the sand
Not catching my dress and tearing it
Not going home with bloody
Nose and elbows

Once I dreamed
To be a world-class kickballer
Always bringing in my teammates
From second base
Winning the game
Claiming the gold
At the kiddie Olympics

I had hoped
To join the team

Wave jumping is my specialty
It is only for women over 60
Who never learned
To swim

My son is so lucky
I had him
>   Vaccinated
>   Educated
>   And gave him swimming lessons
He is unhappy

He doesn't know

That's love

MY GRANDMOTHER

A BOOK

CHAPTER 1

Winter Saturdays unless it is snowing
Really hard Grandmother picks me up
At ten o'clock
Sharp I am always
Ready on time

We drive to the Mall to meet
Her *Walking Grannies* Group

We tie our bandanas and put our sweatshirts
around our waists
We look good as we walk
Two times around the Mall
Then we have lunch and story time
Grandmother says We Must Exercise
To stay strong

I am strong for my Grandmother

CHAPTER 2

In April as soon as it was warm
The *Traveling Grannies* took three grandkids
And a bus all the way
To Cincinnati
We swam in the hotel swimming pool and ate breakfast
In our room
We saw the Underground Railroad Museum and I learned
All about history

I am smart for my Grandmother

CHAPTER 3

The *Gardening Grannies* cleared the lot next door
All the Grannies and Grandkids worked really hard
To clean the bottles and trash out
We were very proud of ourselves
Everything good comes from the dirt
Grandmother said as we planted red hot peppers
And sweet green peppers and scallions
And tomatoes and carrot tops and I secretly
Planted a peach nut
We watered and waited and waited and watered and a carrot flower
Bloomed Grandmother says this is good

I work hard for my Grandmother

CHAPTER 4

While the pinto beans
Cooked for dinner
We took a needle and thread and strung
The skinny red hot peppers
We chopped onions and green peppers
And big red peppers and labeled them and put
Them in the freezer
I beat the two eggs and got to stir the milk
For corn muffins
While the muffins baked Grandmother told me stories
About when she was a little girl

I have the best time when Grandmother picks me up

I love my Grandmother very much

The End

I am 3500 feet above the earth. It is autumn and quite beautiful. I am on my way to Chicago. Next to me, getting his pocket picked, is Ellis Haizlip. Why someone would try to pick a pocket on an airplane is beyond me but it is what we call *The Sixties*, though, in fact, it is now *The Seventies* and everyone is either dead or depressed so I guess people will try anything. Ellis turns to ask the woman if she is trying to pick his pocket. She is indignant. "Then what," he wants to know, "is your hand doing on my behind?" She sits way back. Now he is indignant. My sense of safety has now been breached. The plane hits a CAT, clear air turbulence. I now accept the coming crash. I should never have even been on the plane. Ellis had called to ask if I could or would run over to Chicago with him. He is going to meet Gwendolyn Brooks. "You don't need me to meet Gwendolyn Brooks," I point out. "Yes," he insists, "I do. You have met her. You know all her friends. You are a militant, too. Things will go smoother if you go." "Gwendolyn Brooks is not a militant. You don't need me." "She has an Afro. She works with that gang, the Blackstone Rangers. She is dangerous." "Don't be silly. She's a lovely old lady who will adore you. I'm sure she knows who you are." "I don't want to go alone."

And that was that.

I had met Ms. Brooks when I was in college. She had come to Fisk University for a poetry reading and I was one of the people who was invited to the dinner. I didn't seriously think she had any reason to remember me but Ellis was Ellis. He didn't want to go alone. I think the really stupid thing I said to Ms. Brooks was : "I wrote my 7th grade book report on you and got an A." I don't honestly remember what she said back but the fact that she didn't sort of spit at my feet showed she was a real lady. "It's not as if she and I are friends, Ellis." But he didn't want to go alone.

We visited Gwen at her old homeplace on Cottage Grove. It was a small house with a fence, not picket, around it. She had invited some of OBACI to the encounter. Most of them I did know: Haki Madhubuti, Carolyn Rodgers, Walter Bradford, among others. We all sat in her living room in chairs or on the floor. She had made some snacks. I think Ellis wanted Gwen to appear on *Soul!* which was the television show he hosted. The folk in the room kicked that one around, too. Gwen got up to clear away the dishes and I got up to help. I put what I was carrying in the sink then looked for the right door to open. "Which one is the dishwasher?" I asked since I didn't want to appear meddlesome by opening each cabinet door until I found it. "I don't have a dishwasher," she said. "But the dishes have to be done. Does Mr. Blakely do the dishes?" I was laughing, then. "My Grandmother would never wash dishes. She said she cooked so Grandpapa had to do his share. I didn't know anyone else who did that!" I was enjoying sharing that bit of information. Gwen looked at me like I had lost at least half my mind. "I do the dishes," she said. "But why would you do that?" As if I had lost the other half she said very slowly, "B e c a u s e they are d i r t y." I have to tell you this: Yes. She washed them. But she refused to dry them. She put them away damp. "I never dry dishes because they will dry themselves. But I do wash them."

She was not a good cook either.

She didn't come to New York to do *Soul!* And *Soul!* at that time couldn't go to Chicago to film so it was our loss. Except that for some reason Gwen didn't think I was an idiot. I had written her a thank you note for our evening with her and enclosed my telephone number. I really couldn't think of a single thing a girl with two books published could do for a Pulitzer Prize winner but it was Grandmother's home training that came out. I didn't know then that Gwen is an early riser. And she likes to gossip. My phone would ring at 7:00 A.M. (6:00 A.M. CST) and she would say, as if I didn't know her voice, "It's Gwendolyn. Did I awaken you?" The answer to that is always No but Gwen's children were my age, grown and gone. My child was just out of diapers so any sleep I could get was sorely welcomed. I would scuttle off to get a cup of coffee to see what the news is.

Peter Lawford was one of my favorite public figures not only because he was in happy movies that I liked but also because when all was said and done he was the man who kept the secrets. I admire that.

Finally Gwen was going to Africa. I got an early morning call announcing the news. I sat right up. "How can that be!" I exclaimed. "There is no way they built a highway across the Atlantic Ocean!" "Stop your caterwauling, I'm flying." Gwen was noted for not flying. She and Mari Evans would take a train or bus or be driven. But to go to Africa you had to fly. Or cruise. And if one was scary the other was certainly unacceptable. What's the difference if you fall from the sky or fall into the ocean. She would fly.

She was going with her good friend, Dudley Randall. When they got to New York we had dinner together. Gwen loved that Japanese restaurant that made the food at the table. Dudley mentioned a larger company wanted to purchase Broadside Press. "Wow!" I said. "That's great news." "I'm not going to sell," he said. Gwen asked if I didn't agree. I didn't. "Sell and do something else. Sell and start a gallery. Sell and do whatever but Sell. It's a business decision. Make it." They both looked at me with that look. It was good advice. But no one listens to me. We had fun in New York then they were off to Africa.

Gwen and I shared a birthday with Prince and Allen Iverson and a million other folk. Every year I would open *USA Today* on June 7 to the birthday notice. They would list everybody but Gwen and me. I finally wrote a blistering letter to the Birthday Editor: *I can see why you might not list me as I am not everyone's cup of tea but what excuse do you have not to list*

Pulitzer Prize winner Gwendolyn Brooks, the Poet Laureate of Illinois? I cc'ed Gwen. The next year our birthday fell on a Saturday, then a Sunday. Then she died before she got to see it.

Haki started a Gwendolyn Brooks Festival. I was invited to the second or third one. Gwen came in on Haki's arm in the most beautiful pink St. John dress and Ferragamo shoes. I went *Wow you look great!* **I spent too much money**, she said. *It's never too much when you look this good.* She laughed. *Every girl needs St. John.*

The last time I saw Gwen, Seattle was playing the Bulls in Game 4. A group of us were going to have dinner with her that night but she didn't feel up to it. She invited us by for dessert. When we arrived at the new home on Chicago Beach Drive it was Game time. "Mind if we turn the game on?" we asked. "Of course not," she said. "Who's playing?" "Gwen," I patiently began explaining, "this is important. You must know basketball. How can you be expected to be taken seriously as a black woman if you don't know basketball?" "I know Michael Jordan," she replied quite huffily. "Yes," I said, "but tonight we have to cheer for Seattle." "Oh, no. I can't cheer against Michael." "Well, not against him," I tried to point out, "but for Seattle so that we can let Michael *really* shine in Game 5." When Michael Jordan gets the ball we raise our hands and sway and say "Michael" in a sort of chant. "But tomorrow I can cheer for him?" "Yes." When Mr. Blakeley came in from his studio a bit later the four of us were engrossed in the game chanting "Michael." "How did you get my wife to watch the game let alone cheer?" he asked astonished. "She likes me better than she likes you." I laughed. Of course he knew better.

Saturn had set up a "Thank You" tour to thank Black women for supporting their cars. It was a California to New York tour. Gwen was to join us in Chicago. Dr. B. J. Bolden took Gwen's place onstage. Then her cell phone rang. B. J. announced what we already knew.

Mr. Blakely died sitting in the same chair in which I sat when I had last visited. He was watching a baseball game. I sent flowers to Mari Evans. People remember the family but forget what happens when you lose a friend. A meteor shot upward. There is a poem somewhere in the universe unread unspoken but most definitely felt.

Come here, Rap, let me tell you something. You ain't no orphan. You got folks. You come up from the south with that sweat and that moan. The blues come up a bit before. Brought gospel with it. Everybody singing the blues but it was the children that jump-started the Harlem Renaissance. All that "I've Known Rivers" and "When Miss Sue Wears Red" and "What Is Africa to Me" and all those beautiful words saying how great it is to be black and proud and you don't have to hang your head for nothing. I say you got folks. Your great-grandmother was the Spirituals carrying tales of escape as well as remembering where we came from. I love that old song that says "when I fall on my knees with my face to the rising sun . . ." To the East, don't you see? I love all those songs that tell who we are when some folks wouldn't let us read nor write and they figured we'd forget. No. We did not forget. We do not forget. So, anyway, the work songs and the blues started telling the stories once the freedom came. The blues was the children and again it was Brother Langston who said "You've taken my blues and gone . . . put them on Broadway . . ." But what a lot of people don't know is Broadway itself emerged from uptown cabaret from rent parties which were just more polite juke joints, you see what I mean? And now after rhythm and blues and a bit of funk here and there, you came. Rap, your daddy is the blues; your mama is gospel. That's what they didn't want you to know. They want you to think you're illegitimate but I was there. I saw them jump the broom and I know they loved each other; still do. Some people want to judge it but love is love. You the love child of gospel and the blues. And don't let nobody take that away from you. You belong. As long as you tell the truth, you belong. Yeah, Def Poetry Jam. Rap. Hip-Hop Nation. You belong.

We came to New York as some sort of tail end of the Harlem Renaissance. We poets, playwrights, dancers, singers, seekers of a new way or a better way or in some cases just any way to find a way to live.

We mostly didn't get to Harlem. Some of us went on to Brooklyn; some of us made Village stops, some of us found rent control and rent stabilization on the Upper West Side and tucked in and called it home. I had come from Ohio by way of Tennessee. My nonsegregated experiences were Tri Hi Y, Fellowship Camp and a year at the University of Pennsylvania School of Social Work. I was to begin Columbia U. in the fall.

This is what I most remember: Louis Micheaux had a bookstore on 125th and Seventh. The store is gone and yet remains world famous. Micheaux had put a sign *The Goddamn White Man* at the top of his store and the city tried to make him take it down. Malcolm X had his photo taken in front of that sign. Mr. Micheaux agreed to sell my first book which I had self-printed. Then one of the books was stolen. No one stole from Micheaux so he said to me: You are a real writer. I was bursting with pride. He and Miss Brown and Mrs. Micheaux also invited me for coffee. The beans had come from Africa on the Black Star Line. Very few people drank that coffee as it would eventually run out. And that is Harlem.

There were native New Yorkers like June Jordan and Toni Cade who hung out all over the city. They understood the subway system; they knew the nooks and crannies. They could usually be found in Yvette LeRoi's Liberty Bookstore. The rest of us rode our bikes or walked the city since we didn't like being underground. If you went uptown on Saturday you could find a poetry reading and eventually someone might ask you to read. And since we all read at some point it became a movement and since we were Black it became Black Arts. There really was no leader and it was not really a movement but the ebb and flow of young, talented, ambitious, committed people in an area the size of the Dallas–Ft. Worth Airport which meant we would run into each other now and again.

We all found publishers and radio and television and speaking engagements and competitions. I had self-published an anthology entitled *Night Comes Softly* in which I had asked and received permission to include "If You Saw a Negro Lady" by June Jordan. I didn't have money only books to give. The anthology never did make its money back but I still love it. Then June published *His Own Where* and I published *Gemini* and this is my June Jordan story. The *New York Times Book Review* sent my book to June and June's book to me without telling us. When I received *His Own Where* I read it and liked it all right but something didn't feel quite right. I try to listen to something so I sent it back declining to review since the *NYTimes* hadn't asked me to review anything else for them. June reviewed *Gemini*. Page 3 review. She hated it. Which became embarrassing for her. I totally understood because it was just business. But we are frequently harder on ourselves than others are and communications are short-circuited.

So I was thrilled when the *New York Times Magazine* offered me an opportunity to sing a sister song for June. We are, after all, in the same business of lighting candles, boiling cabbage, baking bread. Maybe a poem will wing its way to the stratosphere where poets go to rest before they come back reincarnated artists trying yet again. But the *NYTimes* said Nobody would understand the poem; it was "too deep." And once again June Jordan and I are separated by the newspaper conglomerate that prints all the news that fits (its idea of news).

It's sort of like dreaming. We reach for some place we maybe haven't explored within ourselves before and we come to this poem, this essay we always wished we had written, this interview we wish we had given, this short story, this novel, this autobiography that we absolutely know will win a prize. Or not. It will make us happy anyway. We look, most humans, for a way to be warm and safe; for a haven for our bodies when, once fire was discovered and clothes invented, when once we understood why the squirrels moved seeds around and what to call the plant the jaguar got giggly off of, when once we no longer worried about being eaten by other mammals or each other we looked for meaning with this life we were given. We are not in the cave position; we are not in some wilderness of the body; we are not being pursued by aliens who will kill us because they are foreign and mean: we are in pursuit of our own fears; we seek to climb the mountain of our own frustrations; we endeavor to overcome our own hatreds. Writing, if we are to think and rethink the possibilities, should make us kinder; should teach us to walk in another's shoes; should open us up to the security that today's task is not just bread on the table and coats on our backs but also patience in our hearts and a seeking of understanding. Since we cannot go everywhere and see everything, books were invented and imaginations soared. And we seek to ride the winds of possibilities. We listen to the stories of villains and heroes. We hear and feel the poetry. We seek newer worlds and other ways.

Some explorers sailed into the African coast to collect the free humans who would be carried through Middle Passage into the New World and made slaves; some explorers who were African and free did not choose to accept the challenge and surrendered to the ocean. Some explorers set sail for the Arctic and fell in love with Penguins and refused to kill them and died for lack of food. Some explorers climbed the highest mountains just to reach the top. Some foraged the woods discovering new mushrooms and new birds and a new possibility for humans. But some explorers used words to uncover the depths of the human heart, the darkness and the light; some explored the unknown and unforgiven to bring the healing light of the sun. Some looked for cures of diseases and some, like poets, looked to define the disease. Madame Curie looked inside the human body; Louis Pasteur looked inside bacteria; and some simply looked at us and said we can do better. There are stamps and proclamations and holidays celebrating those heroes we think of as white. There are few stamps, proclamations, and holidays celebrating those we know to be black.

We will miss June Jordan. For her courage, her insight, her love of us all. We will miss this poet.

FOR THE LYRIC THEATRE

(ON ITS 75TH ANNIVERSARY)

To the mirror that is the story
To the makeup that brings us in
To the staging that points the time
To the lights that bring the magic
To the drama that makes us cry
To the mysteries that take our breath
To the smiles that bring forth laughter
To the glamour that is opening night
To the sadness of the last day
To the reality that without theater
To the reality that without movies
To the reality that without another way of learning
   We would all be the poorer

Let us raise a glass to all theaters

To the understanding that without fantasy
   We would not understand reality

DOORS AND KEYS

(CHOICES)

I'm against prison. It was probably a bad idea hundreds of years
ago when somebody thought it was some sort of progression
over, say, stoning people to death or cutting off hands or branding
or whipping, not to mention stocks or hanging and lynching.
Prison is not a good idea because it puts two people in prison:
the prisoner and the guard. And the rest of us become inheritors
of The Fugitive Slave Law, requiring us to turn in people who
seek their freedom through the Underground Railroad or the
overland express, or face the consequences of the full force of the
law for not doing so. Newspapers, radio, television, and movies
have made us afraid of our fellow citizens who are accused of
being heretics, witches, christians, Jews, Muslims, drug lords,
drug users, prostitutes, sodomites, anything somehow different
from what we think we are or should be but not afraid of slum
lords, union busters, corrupt and graft-taking politicians, insider
traders, employers paying less than minimum wage, college
presidents shutting down debate. But I couldn't articulate that
when I was a child; it's a grown-up thought. All I could do
when I was much younger but old enough to look at the world
was to know, whether or not I could change it, whether or not
it was the way it was, whether or not it would always be that
way: It was wrong. It was wrong to pay the same dime yet have
to walk to the back of the bus. It was wrong to have to pass
a "white" school to go to a "colored" school. It was wrong to
have Colored and White signs. It was wrong that Emmett Till
was murdered. It was wrong that the Sixteenth Street Baptist
Church was dynamited. It was wrong that Medgar Evers was
shot in the back and bled to death in his own driveway. And
whatever was not right could be, if not corrected, then certainly
reproved by people with kinder hearts, better minds and the
courage to speak out for their beliefs. I learned this from my
grandmother.

I could see the doors. Doors have never been a problem
to anyone. If you can't see them you run into them anyway

so you may as well learn to recognize a door when it's there. Otherwise you spin your wheels and blame yourself for things that, actually, have nothing to do with you. Let's say you are beaten up in the school yard if not every day then regularly. You begin to think that you can do something to stop it. You might cryptically mention it to your parents or maybe a teacher you like. But you can see no one is going to actually do anything about it. You have to fight your own battle. Most likely you will not win. Your clothes will be torn and your nose bloodied but one thing will happen. They will stop beating you up. And taking your lunch money. And here's the trick. They will want to be what is now called "your friend." Don't do it. You still hate them. They still do not mean you well. All you did was fight to be left alone.

Or, let's say, your parents argue and sometimes fight on weekends. You read up on parental fighting and recognize it is a result of a clash of responsibilities. Your father is being artificially held down by racial prejudice; your mother has no way to make that better. He, in what can only be considered a cowardly way, takes it out on the person who cares about him. Whatever it is that they have, it is clear they understand each other or perhaps like each other or at least are so committed to each other that they will not change. What takes the longest to figure out is: It has nothing to do with you. They will not break up because of you; they do not stay together because of you. So you have to negotiate this space that makes you very nervous. You scratch your dandruff until your scalp bleeds. You learn to distrust the night. And are very cautious during the day. Any loud voice makes you jump. And look for something. That will do damage. Everybody thinks you are cute. And smart. And lucky to be who you are. Of course your mother has taught you what goes on in this house stays in this house. And you would actually be ashamed except you have read enough to know that if there is shame it does not belong to you. It is neither your shame nor your mother's and perhaps not even your father's that everyone is crowded into too tight a space and someone has to exhale. You, nonetheless, understand this cannot be good for you. It is a door you are unable to open. You cannot squeeze through. You cannot climb over the transom. You cannot slide under. You need a key.

Train fare to Knoxville is $10.50. Cab fare to the train station is about $5.00. Maybe something for a sandwich another $5.00. Luckily you have a Godmother and unluckily she has died. But luckily she left $100.00 to you which when you consider she worked as a cook and took care of herself and her husband and I should point out that she was a cook not a caterer nor a chef so the fact that she could leave anything is astonishing but that she left it to you is a godsend. You have to walk about five miles to the bank and five miles back. Though you are only fourteen it is still your money and the bank gives you your $25.00 because you thought it was better to have more than you need than less. You go back home and pack a very small suitcase. You were going to leave a note because you never ever like having to discuss unpleasant things with anyone but you decide that is the cowardly way so you hide your suitcase under your bed and wait until everyone is home, has dinner and is sitting in an apparently good mood. You then casually mention you would like to go visit your grandmother and your father asks your mother has she spoken to "Lou." No but she can call. I called, you volunteer, and she said it would be all right. You neglected to tell her you want to stay, and you certainly neglected to tell them, as everyone would feel they should dissuade you because after all they do love you which you know, and do want you, which you know, it's just that this thing that rises up on the weekends is more than you can comprehend and even in the comprehending you know you need to get away from it or you will be just like it. Your mother points out that she gets paid Friday and your father offers to take you to the train station which is about a twenty-mile ride and you smile because the one thing you don't want is to be home when the weekend comes. So the next morning after you have washed the dishes and done a little dusting and tried to straighten things up so that when everyone gets home it will not be like you didn't care but like you needed to leave, you call Mr. Gray who runs a taxi service and he picks you up and for the $5.00 you thought it would be takes you to the train station and you are on the afternoon train to Knoxville. And your grandmother. And safety.

And I'm still not sure if that's a choice like I chose to go to college or I chose to be a writer or I choose always as best I can to keep truth and compassion in my life. It seems most decisions are a lack of choice. A back against the wall. A flashlight with dead batteries in the night. A parachute that just has to open since you are already in free fall. And maybe it doesn't. Maybe the monsters come from under the bed. Maybe you are crushed against the wall. But I still do know this: You have to be who you think you are. And you can't give up on that or you will become what you don't want to be. All we do is make decisions within the choices which are not always and necessarily of our choosing. All we can do, I believe, is take the love and give the love and try to remember who dreamed dreams of us. And try to be faithful to that.

When winter blows the north wind over my pond the fish go deeper seeking calmer spaces not from fear but from the understanding that fish should not tackle winds . . . fish should go deeper . . . fish should seek different meanings

It would be unusual for winds to consider all the seeds on their backs . . . it would be wonderful . . . but unusual . . . for winds to worry . . . winds blow . . . fish seek deeper spaces . . . and you and I find warmth inside

No one knows what warm means . . . heat being the "absence of cold" sort of like satisfaction being the absence of hunger or war the absence of peace . . . subtracting . . . taking away . . . negative definitions are insufficient because winter winds blow . . . and fish swim deeper . . . and you and I find warmth inside . . . which is more than the absence of outside

Inside speaks of friendship . . . and homemade ice cream . . . and cookies . . . and orange juice . . . and laughter . . . and a writers' group . . . that lives . . . inside . . . us . . . all

BRAVE MAN DANCING

(FOR RICHARD FEWELL)

When brave men dance
Who sings

When courageous men bask in that midnight sun
Who understands their pain

When men of hope and men of dreams write poems
Who listens

Who listens to the beat

Of a brave man dancing

The sun does not so much set . . . as the earth moves to another
position . . . change . . . while normal . . . is neither necessarily
welcomed nor good . . . we should climb mountains . . . not to
diminish them . . . but to elevate ourselves

The sum of all love . . . is forgiveness

When will we learn . . . what can make us remember . . .
imagination is the future . . . dreams are the only reality . . .
when power corrupts . . . John F. Kennedy said . . . poetry
cleanses

And doors close . . . while windows open . . . Some are
hired . . . some are fired . . . All give an honest day's work . . .
somereceiveanhonestday'spay . . . Someplay . . . Somepray . . .
Sophistication . . . not love . . . is the answer . . . to hate

Poetry . . . is the antidote . . . to arrogance

A DAUGHTER COMES HOME

(FOR MARVALENE HUGHES UPON ACCEPTING
THE PRESIDENCY OF DILLARD UNIVERSITY)

When daughters leave home
they take a bit of the light
most of the sunshine
all the giggly laughter

Of course we never say:
    Don't go
We say:
      You need your education
      That man you love
      He may not treat you
      Right

When daughters leave
home it's not like when
sons
do

Sons go off to seek
fame or a fortune or some sort of medal
we know they will not
be back
whole:
      Maybe broken by war
      Maybe Positive for love
      Maybe in bits and pieces
         from all the vultures who pluck
         at their hopes and dreams

When sons leave home
      they are gone

But daughters return
  To air the quilts
    of winter night sweats
  To clean the cellars
    of old peach preserves
  To make mothers buy
    red dresses
  To cajole fathers
    who suffered strokes on the job
    to go to a baseball game
  To rear their children
    and bury the dog

Daughters return to retire
    an ancient debt
    that says:
    Those who have loved and protected me
    will now be loved and protected

A daughter comes home
    to cook and wash and laugh so hard
    to straighten out and straighten up
    to tell stories to listen to tales
Heaven peeks down to applaud
    and the angels
    sing

BROTHER BROTHER BROTHER

(THE ISLEY BROTHERS OF LINCOLN HEIGHTS)

You see . . . I know the Isley Brothers. Know where they come from. Know the high school they went to. Remember when they moved to Blue Ash. Knew their little brother Vernon who used to do a mad and wonderful itch. And who remembers the itch? But Vernon would stand onstage and reach around and swizzle his hips and the amateur night audience would be on their feet though Rudolph and O'Kelly were probably the beneficiaries of that energy but . . . you see . . . I know them

You see . . . We all come from Lincoln Heights which is an independent Black city just outside Cincinnati and we mostly say we are from Cincinnati because nobody knows Lincoln Heights but back in the old days when white people would periodically go crazy and need-want-have to kill somebody Black lots of Black people moved from the river-front into the West End and when they could if they could out of the West End and into the Valley and in the Valley . . . you see . . . land was ten cents an acre which is not a lot today but from folks walking away from slavery and folks running from crazy folks who wanted to-needed to-were definitely going to- kill them ten cents meant the difference between life and death . . . But

You see . . . It's like everything else so Black folks moved way out there and the Erie Canal was supposed to go from Cleveland down what ultimately became I-75 to connect the Lake to the River and if that had happened instead of it not happening then all the Black folks who scraped together a nickel or so so that they could get a little piece of land would have had worthless condemned land but the canal did not happen though Lincoln Heights did

And then wars and stuff started happening and General Electric where progress is the most important product wanted to have a lot of land but they didn't want to have to pay for it so they split the land and called it Evendale and what was left on the hill was Lincoln Heights and I'm sure I don't have to say which is Black and which is white but I bet you can guess . . . So

You see . . . The Valley Homes were built for folks to work in the GE plant not to mention folks needing some place to live and other folks not wanting to live near them though the Valley Homes were good enough for us which considering the alternative they were but they doesn't make it right but it was definitely okay because Lincoln Heights had great athletes who would have been famous if they had been allowed to go to desegregated schools so Virgil Thompson went to West Virginia State but nobody much cared about talented boys from a small Black town that was incorporated and he came back

You see . . . We had singers too and Pookey Smith could really sing and everybody loved to hear him at Christmas or any other time but Pookey and his brother didn't have a mother like Mrs. Isley who was determined that her boys were going to get out not because she didn't like Lincoln Heights or even the Valley Homes but she knew if she could get them out then the talents they had would have a chance to grow and that's more or less when they moved to Blue Ash and Vernon was run over by a car and all of Lincoln Heights wanted to see them become rich and famous since we already knew they were talented and beautiful. But Ernie came along and we all were happy though nobody does the itch anymore since that's what Vernon did . . . And we all remembered

You see . . . When they started perfecting *SHOUT* and Mrs. Isley said she was taking her boys to New York and Elaine said she was going with Rudolph and Ronald used to date my sister but she had to go on to college and the Isleys know because . . . you see . . . they are from Lincoln Heights that they had to take care of each other and they have done that . . . We all mourned when O'Kelly now called Kelly died because he was such a good friend to all of us and none of them ever forgot where they came from and how much love all of Lincoln Heights still sends out to all of them and just recently

You see . . . I was home and it was Mother's Day at church and their Grandmother wanted to sing a tribute and she was still doing that Isley *SHOUT* at 92 and a lot of other people did that Isley *SHOUT* like the Beatles and Joey Dee and stuff but it was the Isley *SHOUT* that was our thing and other than the Beatles they have sold the most records . . . and Lincoln Heights

You see . . . Always knew they were special and that's why we know *Brother Brother Brother* may be an album title but it is a way of life with these powerful, wonderful sons of Lincoln Heights who are Brother to us all . . . don'cha know

JACKIE ROBINSON IS DEAD

Things get set
In motion
That cannot be
Undone

Salt in water can
Be distilled
Out
Burned photos
Cannot be
Reconstructed
The genie having left
The jar
Will not return
To be content
To wait
To be discovered
To be rubbed
And made over
Since after all
She really just
Wants us to love her

No!
No!
No!
The genie is not
The image seared
In your imagination
We no longer
Care
What you think
Or why

Jackie Robinson
Is dead
And if you touch
Ron Artest
He will kick
Your
ass

FOR CLEVELAND "PEPI" PARKER 3RD

(FATALLY STRUCK BY A STRAY BULLET)

Baseballs fly
On cloudless days
    purposeful
    hopeful
    determined
    Forever
Young
Exuberant
Instructive

This is for the men . . . the men with hopes and dreams and talents . . . that sometimes other men find ways to use and use and use up . . . and when the men are used up they are discarded . . . like so many Christmas toys that don't work or maybe like Easter eggs that have teeny tiny cracks . . . not enough cracks so that the Easter bunny and his crew refuse to dye them . . . they . . . after all . . . look so lovely when scattered across the lawn in all their many colors but . . . well . . . that teeny tiny crack is just enough to sort of say *sure you can find this pretty egg and maybe put it in your basket for a while but don't you know that little crack means one day it will stink* . . . that one day whatever it is that makes eggs break open . . . whatever it is that snuggles inside . . . whatever it is that wants . . . needs . . . has . . . to get out . . . will break this shell causing a stink . . . this is for the men

This is for the men . . . the men who knew the difference between cutting bait . . . and fishing . . . and who having been carted away from all known waters . . . found a way to fish . . . anyway . . . like the women found a way . . . to quilt . . . like we all found a way . . . to maintain integrity . . . this is for the men who were sent back . . . for a reason . . . or no reason . . . this is for the men who ran . . . and tackled . . . and threw their bodies . . . to block the way . . . and no body ever really said Thank You . . . no everybody assumed . . . this made them happy . . . never ever knowing what makes men happy . . . other men claimed some kind of right . . . some kind of contracts . . . some kind of waivers . . . on the dreams of the men who dreamed

This is for equality . . . men and women . . . blacks and whites . . . jews and arabs . . . oriental-occidental . . . dreamers and the blind . . . brilliant and the dumb . . . all equal because we have decided . . . they are equal . . . it's a good system . . . make a decision . . . don't lynch anybody in Springfield Missouri or Indianapolis Indiana . . . don't shoot anybody in the back while he is reaching for his wallet to show you he lives there and please please don't rape immigrants with broomsticks in New York City . . . don't run a firing line on women sleeping in cars . . . quit picking the brown . . . the red . . . and itinerant poets for random searches all the time . . . try not to tie young gay men to posts and beat them until their brains are jelly . . . try to resist the urge to drag James Byrd behind your pickup truck . . . lay a headstone for Emmett Till in Money Mississippi and on the steps of the Lincoln Memorial in Washington DC build a life-size statue . . . head rag and all . . . standing tall . . . showing off that killer smile of Tupac Shakur since he too freed the slaves . . . Lincoln only in body in states he did not control . . . Tupac all over this planet where his truth reached . . . both were shot down . . . by the same evil forces . . . hiding in bushes . . . and running away . . . this is for equality . . . because we made a decision

And this is definitely for the good men . . . the good men who when knocked down . . . got up again . . . to go just one more round . . . or show somebody else how to do it . . . this is for the good men who planted their dreams in the hearts of other young men . . . this is for the good men who went back home with their heads held high . . . who look for ways to bend the light . . . and shine it on the young men . . . the new dreamers . . . the talented . . . hopeful . . . strong young men . . . who reap the dreams . . . and plant some dreams . . . because the best of the good men . . . are the dreams of all men . . . so this is for Coach Reamon . . . who talked that talk . . . and walked that walk . . . and dreamed of change . . . this is for Coach Reamonwhoknows Diamondsinthe Rougharestilldiamonds . . . still unusual . . . very rare . . . but always precious . . . This is definitely for holding on . . . Yeah . . . for holding on

HAIKU

A LOVE POEM TO POETRY

The words dance
In the poet's heart
Making her
Sing

DON'T HOLD ME BACK

(FOR WINFRED REMBERT)

And when I dream I dream
In colors
Even rainy days sparkle
Even clouds have shine

And when I hope I hope
In smiles
Even laughter has bubbles
Even giggles ballet

And so I understand
That life is precious
And important
And wonderful

When things go wrong
When things go back
When things don't work

I start to dream

THE FIRST DREAM

(FOR THE MARY MCLEOD BETHUNE
PERFORMING ARTS CENTER)

Mrs. Bethune had the First Dream
That people who looked
Like her *could* dream
That people whose people had toiled
Unpaid unappreciated unwanted though sought
Could take the time to reflect

Mrs. Bethune had the First Dream
That kindness and caring and love
Could be taught
That people whose people had toiled could take
The time to contemplate
Possibilities

Mrs. Bethune had the First Dream
That art and beauty
That sanctuary and solace
Could come to the people
Whose people had toiled

And we dedicate this realization
To that First Dream

And while awake

We dream on

P.O. BOX 2491
ROANOKE, VA 24010

Dear Sir:

Can you please tell me what WDBJ thinks it is doing? Television stations are here to serve the public. S E R V E.

Saturday morning my 85-year-old mother arose early, had a hearty breakfast, read her *Roanoke Times* (though she saves *The Current* and the comics for her bedtime reading), and settled in her den for the Tech game.

My phone blared at 8:04 A.M. On a Saturday no less. She was in a low grade panic. "I can't find the game!" she cried. My mother is almost deaf. I have been trying to get her qualified for that telephone that prints out a message but no luck so far. I know she cannot hear anything I might say so I have to get up, get dressed, and get into that flow of molasses they call "game day traffic" so that I can explain to her: "It's not on TV. They aren't broadcasting it."

"But why," she cried. "It's sold out." I try to explain: "They don't think it's much of a game."

"What do they mean—much?" she asks.

"Well, they think Tech will run over FAMU."

"Yes!" She gleefully clapped her hands.

"They think the score will be in the high double digits, maybe fifty or more, to zero."

"Absolutely! Yes! That's what I think, too!"

"Well, that's not much of a game."

"These people are nuts! That's a great game! Tech up by thirty or forty points at halftime? That's great! Then you can relax and enjoy it. What is it with those folks who want those one and two point competitions? That just wears me out. I go to bed so tired I can't sleep well."

I try to explain that some folk don't look at it the same way she does. But she is extremely unhappy. She spent Saturday afternoon looking longingly at her darkened giant surround-a-sound screen muttering more to herself than to me "I just don't understand." Then she realized what she had to do. "Will you take me to WDBJ?" "Why?" I cautiously asked. "I want to picket them." I was able to dissuade her from such a drastic act this time but I'm not sure how long I can hold her off. I know she has sorority friends and senior friends who feel the same way she does. She agreed to hold off if I would agree to write a letter.

Let this be a warning. Virginia Tech football games should be shown. Or you just might have to answer to the Senior Brigade.

Sincerely,

NIKKI GIOVANNI

FOR YOLANDE GIOVANNI

THE OLD LADIES GIVE A PARTY

The lamb sickles
The corn relish (that little bit Uncle Clinton left for the rest of us)
The ribs
The sliced smoked steak
The baked beans
My very own pound cake (that I didn't have to share)
That wonderful homemade ice cream
The refreshing champagne
The nice warm red wine
Don't forget the little bitty corn muffins
The fun
The sisterhood
Ahhhhhh another birthday
That's what I mean . . . good for us
And many mooooooooooore!

HOTEL ROOMS

The quiet simplicity
   of a hotel room
Nothing more than you need
   nothing less

A bed
   usually king size
A desk
   with easy chair
Remote color TV
   with The Deuce
   to boot
Clean towels twice
   a day
Room Service coffee
   and a newspaper
   with intruding headlines
Life could be more
   difficult
But certainly not more
   comfortable
Than a hotel room
Where poems come
   Spinning
   Dancing
   Teasing
   Daring
You
   To write
   them

THE MOST WONDERFUL SOUP IN THE WORLD

Soup, where I come from, is sacred . . . the food of the gods . . .
the most wonderful thing on Earth to eat because it is so hard
to make. Canned soups and frozen soups and soups that you
add water to and stir and I'm sure I don't even have to men-
tion microwave soups are not allowed in the house. My grand-
mother always told me the reason ghosts come back is some-
body is either opening a can of soup or making a box cake. It
was the very longest time before I realized ghosts could come
back for other reasons.

My mother, who is without doubt the world's best bean
cooker, makes a mean soup, too. You need to know a couple
of things about Mommy and me before I share this recipe.
Mommy likes to save things. I'm sure it goes back to grand-
mother. I don't. I'm sure it goes back to my father. My father
was always single-mindedly focused. If he was polishing his
shoes he'd just as soon take the tail of his good shirt to finish
the shine. That drove Mommy crazy. I'm sort of like that.
Mommy, on the other hand, will split a sheet of paper towel in
half to get double the use and if she only used the half she used
to do something like mop up a bit of water, she'd spread it on
the countertop to dry and be used again. I moved back home
because my father was diagnosed with colon cancer. So what
we have is two women in one kitchen. Yo! A recipe for Frontier
Soup or a recipe for disaster.

See, Mommy believes in saving grease. Grease. G R E A S E.
Unbelievable. I don't do leftovers and especially not grease.
I don't even cook with it. I would, therefore, throw the bacon
grease out. She would hide it in the back of the fridge. I would
find it and throw it out. She moved her can under the sink. We
played that game for a couple of months. I trying to convert her
to olive oil; she tying to convert me to . . . grease. Now Edna
Lewis, whom I love, says you should cook with lard. Mommy
pasted that article up all over the kitchen. But Miss Lewis,
I tried to explain, means fresh lard. Fresh, smesh, lard is grease

and grease is flavor. What is her book called? In Search of Olive Oil? I could fight Mommy. I could fight Grandmother. I could, if actually called to do so, fight Edna Lewis. I might even stand toe-to-toe with Scott Peacock. But not all of them at once. I was defeated. If I had to keep the grease I would organize it.

I went downstairs and found a really beautiful large jar. I had, at one point, considered keeping pennies in it or goldfish but now it was going to work for a higher cause: leftovers. If she was keeping grease then I would keep a little snippet of whatever we ate. At first it was potatoes. I love boiled potatoes; they are, indeed, a gift from the gods. Then it was a bit of the roast, a bit of the chicken, a snippet of the pork chops. There were green things: green beans, greens, okra because I eat okra at least once a week, asparagus. My jar was filling up. There were squashes: zucchini, yellow squash, the squash with the neck. Eggplant, turnips, parsnips. We looked around at the end of the month and the jar was almost full. Let's make soup we said almost simultaneously. I ran to get a can of beer. There simply is no better starter. We emptied the leftover jar; we added one heaping tablespoon of grease (and by mutual agreement threw the rest away), a large onion, two large carrots, cut up green peppers, a head of garlic because there isn't any such thing as too much of a good thing. We added a large can of whole tomatoes, cut up some hot and sweet peppers, and went away. It cooked on low all afternoon. Periodically one of us would check to see if we should add water or beer . . . both work. At dinner time we set a beautiful table . . . hot crusty bread with pesto for dipping. And the-end-of-the-month-best-soup-in-the-world soup. I gotta tell you my son hated it. We made this dish once a month for all the time we lived together. My father liked it because it had so many flavors and textures. He thought it looked good but then he was sick. Gus, my father, would say Oh is the month over already? And appear utterly delighted. Thomas would say:

Oh No! Not that soup again. Which just goes to show: there's no accounting for taste.

The key to this soup is courage. Mix and match your leftovers. That which cannot be made wonderful with beer will definitely yield to white wine. If all else fails: add milk and call it stew.

MY FIRST MEMORY (OF LIBRARIANS)

This is my first memory:
A big room with heavy wooden tables that sat on a creaky
     wood floor
A line of green shades—bankers' lights—down the center
Heavy oak chairs that were too low or maybe I was simply
     too short
          For me to sit in and read
So my first book was always big

In the foyer up'four steps a semicircular desk presided
To the left side the card catalog
On the right newspapers draped over what looked like
     a quilt rack
Magazines face out from the wall

The welcoming smile of my librarian
The anticipation in my heart
All those books—another world—just waiting
At my fingertips

A POEM FOR MY LIBRARIAN, MRS. LONG

(YOU NEVER KNOW WHAT TROUBLED
LITTLE GIRL NEEDS A BOOK)

At a time when there was no tv before 3:00 P.M.
And on Sunday none until 5:00
We sat on front porches watching
The jfg sign go on and off greeting
The neighbors, discussing the political
Situation congratulating the preacher
On his sermon

There was always radio which brought us
Songs from wlac in nashville and what we would now call
Easy listening or smooth jazz but when I listened
Late at night with my portable (that I was so proud of)
Tucked under my pillow
I heard nat king cole and matt dennis, june christy and ella fitzgerald
And sometimes sarah vaughan sing black coffee
Which I now drink
It was just called music

There was a bookstore uptown on gay street
Which I visited and inhaled that wonderful odor
Of new books
Even today I read hardcover as a preference paperback only
As a last resort

And up the hill on vine street
(The main black corridor) sat our carnegie library
Mrs. Long always glad to see you
The stereoscope always ready to show you faraway
Places to dream about

Mrs. Long asking what are you looking for today
When I wanted *Leaves of Grass* or alfred north whitehead
She would go to the big library uptown and I now know
Hat in hand to ask to borrow so that I might borrow

Probably they said something humiliating since southern
Whites like to humiliate southern blacks

But she nonetheless brought the books
Back and I held them to my chest
Close to my heart
And happily skipped back to grandmother's house
Where I would sit on the front porch
In a gray glider and dream of a world
Far away

I love the world where I was
I was safe and warm and grandmother gave me neck kisses
When I was on my way to bed

But there was a world
Somewhere
Out there
And Mrs. Long opened that wardrobe
But no lions or witches scared me
I went through
Knowing there would be
Spring

IT'S
SPRING

Redbud
Jonquils
Robins on the wing
Dogwood in full bloom
of course it is

it's Spring

HOW YOU GONNA SAVE 'EM? 3RD STANZA

I say how can you save 'em
If they refuse to pray
Let 'em snap their fingers
Let 'em tap their toes
Let 'em wear a bright red wig
With shimmies on their clothes
Diamonds in their teeth
Flowers in their hair
Love enough to make 'em happy
Troubles they can bear
Melodies and belly laughs
Something they can share

RAID THIS JOINT

Canasta . . . Bid Whist . . . Coon Can. . . . Spades . . . Come on,
     Somebody
Raid this joint

Fried fish . . . hush puppies . . . red pepper flakes over thin
     sliced onions
Hard fried chicken wings . . . resting on white bread . . .
     Chitlins simmering for Sister Sadie

Blues from the radio . . . slow dragging from the box . . .
     hands clapping . . . thighs slapping
Singing with the masters

Sweat . . . dancing . . . jokes . . . laughing . . . Saturday
     night thanksgiving
Come on, Somebody . . . I say Somebody Come On
Come on over here
And Raid This Joint

I'M AN AMERICAN

I want a pill

I love Mexico:
     its beautiful people
     its sea turtle policy
     its beaches

I want a pill

"take two pills each morning
for two weeks in Acapulco"
speak Spanish before you
go home

I'm an American
I demand a pill:
     Eat all you want
     Never exercise
     Extra red wine
     Chocolate 'til it tans you

"take two pills each morning"
lose twenty pounds before
your vacation

I'm an American! I tell you!

I want everything

The easy way

"take two pills and war is over"
cheney-bush is a bad dream
I am in love
And I hit
The Lottery

It's my right

I'm an American

BLUES FOR LOVE

I try so hard
To brush my gums
But always end up
On my tongue

It's like a walk
Becomes a run

And counting two
Gets stuck on one

I mean there's something wrong
With me
I need to find
A remedy

Maybe I'll go to the Mall
And buy myself
A love

Usually meals make sense. They have a theme; they are balanced as to nutrition and color. Flavors complement each other. But in the summer you really have to ask: who cares? I like to go to the outdoor market to see what is just plucked from the ground or picked from the trees. I always start with the corn. Bicolored. Small. I usually get a dozen ears but I eat them only four at a time. Then I move on to the potatoes. If it were fall or winter I would never do corn and potatoes in the same meal but it's summer. I look for the little potatoes. The smallest ones to be found. One pint of those. Then beets. I can eat beets every day but summer beets are so tender and smell so earthy. Two bunches, please. My mother says when I was little I would go out into the field next to our house and eat wild onions. She said I would come home just reeking of them. I still love onions. And elephant garlic. A bunch of onions. Just one elephant garlic. About the middle of August the beans start to appear. I love October beans but I will always put them aside for Cranberry Beans. Yes, they are expensive but look at what you get! One package. By now I am at the tomato lady. I love heirloom tomatoes. And German. And Rutgers. And yellow. And green. And cherry. And most especially green ones to fry. A quick wriggle of the nose says the semolina is ready. It usually doesn't come up until 10:00 A.M. but some mornings you get lucky. Since I am now loaded down I can get only a few peaches. People seem to really be enjoying the white peaches but I still like the yellow. Back to the car to unload and head home when I remember: little baby brussels sprouts. That's it. Home to make lunch.

Beets: Wash and rub with olive oil. Bake in oven until tender. I know that only adds to the heat but it's worth it. Pop them out of their skin when done. Slice and put in skillet with plenty of butter. Let them enjoy the butter until you are ready to serve.

Elephant garlic: Since you have the oven on, you may as well bake the garlic. Cut the top off, exposing the cloves.

Drizzle olive oil and a sprinkle few fresh herbs of your choice. Wrap in aluminum foil. Serve on a piece of bread. Use your crab fork to retrieve the cloves. Squeeze garlic bulb when the cloves are gone over the bread. Yummy!

Corn: Shuck and boil. Serve with lots of butter, house made pepper (black pepper, cloves, nutmeg, red peppers, green and red fresh ground peppercorns), a little sea salt. (The better the salt the better the taste.)

Potatoes: Wash but don't peel. Boil until skins crack. Douse with butter. A bit of salt and house made pepper. Shave a small truffle over them.

Brussels sprouts: Trim outer leaves and bottoms. Cut sprouts in half. Melt a bit of butter in a skillet. Sauté sprouts. Turn and add a bit of nutmeg. Move sprouts around to absorb but do not overcook. Just before serving add a splash of brandy and flame.

Green tomatoes: One tomato. Slice very thin. Dip in any soft-shell crab fry solution. Shake excess off. Heat vegetable oil in skillet. When hot put tomatoes in. While they are frying:

Slice one each of your other tomatoes. Arrange beautifully. Drizzle a bit of olive oil, your good salt, and house made pepper. Slice your peaches. Add just a hint of sugar. Slice your semolina bread.

Pour a glass of champagne (or do as I do and drink blanc de blanc) and INDULGE. After all, these are the dog days of summer. You've got a right to spoil yourself.

SERIOUS POEMS

(FOR AMIRI BARAKA AND, MOST ESPECIALLY,
HIS GENTLE SISTER, KIMAKO)

Poems are not advertisements braying
For the good life
They have serious work to do
Birthing people burying people
Celebrating joy mourning loss
Poems are not beer commercials
Or there to really show you which soap
To use
Poems have serious business to do
They need to bring down presidents who
Start wars they themselves wouldn't go to
They need to expose lies about chemical weapons
They need to raise real questions about who flew the planes
Into the world trade center towers
Last most poems knew about it
Computers fly planes and pilots keep
The stews on their knees and smoke cigarettes
Since the cockpit is the only smoking area of the plane
Poems have serious work to do
Since they can't plant okra or tomatoes
They can't brew a beer
Or properly ferment wine
They have to at least recognize the importance of the people
Who sweat whether it is a fireman
A policeman
Or any number of athletes who bring such pleasure
When our team wins
Poems have to tell the truth
Which is world holding up time
They need to remind people of our sacred duty
To remember the captured people whom we called
Slaves
To remember they believed in tomorrow
They believed in us

They believed in the power of a serious poem
To carry our story forward
Poems are serious business
And only serious people
Should apply

There is really only one thing to say to young writers:

Know who you are writing for and to.

I know I write for my Grandmother and the women of The Garden Club and the women of The Book Club and the women of The Missionary Society and the women who are the Usher Board and the women who cook for the Special Sundays and the women who cleaned the pastor's house when his wife was in the hospital and all the women who picketed Rich's Department Store and all the women who sacrificed to send money to Montgomery and especially all the women who cried when Emmett's body was raised from the river and all the women who decried THIS could not and should not happen again.

Because knowing who you want to be proud of you can make all the difference in the world.

Not at all that I don't want others to read my poems or essays. I really would like everyone to read or to hear me but I cannot really know what that will mean so I'll just stick to what I do know.

I want my Grandmother and her friends to look at my work and be pleased. I want the women who endured slavery and the black laws and all the dreams down the drain because their husbands were riddled with bullets and their sons were lynched and they knew they had to stand because if they didn't stand then all that death was in vain. So I know only one thing:

It is important to know who
You want to be proud of you.

And then you can know that you have done all you can do. And you can be proud of your work.

AMERICAN CONVERSATION

Starbucks American Conversation
In which I am glad to add my bit
Of poetic advice for young poets:

Hot allusions
Metaphors over easy
Side order of rhythm
Grit/s plain or with sauce
    Message:
If you want to be a poet
You've got to eat right

THE YELLOW JACKET

We pause in our day
Before completion of evening
Chores
I to cook dinner
And you . . . I'm not sure
What you do

I empty the birdbaths
Always worrying
A virus or germ
Or unpleasant bacteria may lurk
To do fatal harm
To those who only bring
Their voices in joy
And thanksgiving for fresh water

And you buzz and . . . quite frankly . . . annoy
Me as I go about this duty
Fulfilling a contract that was
Never signed and is not at all
Enforceable
But nonetheless a cheerful
Duty to our feathered friends

Recognizing each tree gone
Each bush removed for a deck
Or a patio has left a place
Less welcoming I hope
The birds accept this clean water
As a suitable replacement

I swat at you worried
You will sting
Causing my throat to swell

Blocking my air or
Some other unknown danger
Hurmans attribute when we hear
Buzzes

You wait . . . buzz by . . .
And wait again
Until the water is filled
Where you can sit
Majestically on the edge
And drink

We are not friends
The yellow jacket and I
You will not be tamed
Or trained
Your sound will offer no comfort
Nor your numbers any sense
Of safety

Yet in this evening
Watching you drink
I am in awe
Of your self-possessed
beauty

TEN FOR TONI

(CONGRATULATIONS AND HAPPY ANNIVERSARY)

If our last ten years could go
The same as our first ten years
We'd have only the in-between years
On our own to make our way

If we could anticipate
With the same joy we were anticipated
We'd have only the middle anxieties
To cushion the falls

When we look at the lean years
That brought the good years
When our hands dug the rich soil
To plant our learning seeds

We know any ten years
Are the right years
When love
Waters the garden

DRINKING SNOWFLAKES

It was the coldest day
of winter
            snow swirled
            like the wind was playing
            catch with the trees
Jennifer dressed in a hurry:
She put on
            wool long under johns
            a silk undershirt
            her red cotton turtleneck shirt
            her flannel-lined blue jeans
She put her silk
            sox liners on her feet
            her cotton knee sox over those
            and her feet into her fleece-lined boots
Grabbing
            her heavy snow jacket
            her wool airplane hat with extra ear straps
            and her wool mittens
She came to the breakfast table

Mother had made
oatmeal . . . wheat toast . . . bacon . . . and fried apples

Jennifer ate quickly
because she wanted to meet her friends
and build snowmen
"You didn't drink your orange juice," said Mother
as Jennifer hurried for the door
buttoning and snapping and making sure
she was warmly enough dressed
"It's okay," said Jen, "I'll drink the snowflakes"

And off she went.

WHEN RAINBOWS LAUGH

(FOR ASHLEY BRYAN)

When rainbows laugh
it tickles the sun
who drops jelly beans
on the strawberry's run

The bluebirds fly down
to pick at the leaves
and being well reared
they always say "Please"

And cumulus clouds
who are watching the scene
fog all the way down
to sneak all the green
lemon-lime drops they can find

But something is wrong
clouds can't stay green long
they are white or pink or gray

While washing their hands
they wet all the lands
and everyone scurries away

The butterflies
and baby birds
and moths
and little skunks, too

All run to stay dry
till the clouds pass by
and a rainbow comes
into view

The rainbow laughs
and it tickles the sun
and the sunbeams come out to play

While Ashley smiles
and pulls out his brushes
and paints all the colors
all day

A PROMISE OF SPRING

Summer things
Like childhood giggles
Must be put away

The old swing set
That will need painting
Next year

The fishing rod that sort
Of didn't work

Grandmother embraced
Heaven
While the earth was still
Warm and moist

Woolen blankets and quilts
Are aired
To let the mothballs go

Soon will be the first snow
Flake indicating the season
Of Thanks
The Giving of Christmas
And most especially the promise
Of Spring

WE WRITE

Writing is a frozen
Thought brought
To paper heated
By passions tempered
By sympathy defined
By facts colored
By desire

Words landing
On pages scramble
To arrange thoughts
Giggle and say exactly
What they want ignoring
Us the writers

Our job is to tame
These words
To train them to perform
Properly and should they
Be unable to actually do
The job at least
Come to work
On time and offer
Proper apologies
When they fall short

We learn to negotiate
That space between
Imagination and possibility
Reality and probability
We mold the world
Into our thoughts
Our thoughts mold
Us into a different
Perspective

We seek and hide
We break and mend
We teach and learn
We write

MASKS

(F O R   J E R E   H O D G I N S)

Come on . . . let's jump
High . . . high . . . higher
Let's jump so high everyone will say
Oh, I have never seen anyone jump that high
And we will smile
And take a bow

Or no
Let's put lots of lovely makeup on
Let's paint our cheeks
And fluff our hair
And drape a lovely lovely velvet
Gown around us
We will be Kings and Queens

Quick

Get the crowns
Get the jewels
Don't forget we need manicures
And we will be Kings and Queens
And everyone will say
I have never seen such lovely
Kings and Queens

But no we can be cripples
We can sing a cripple song
Of forgiveness
We will make it all right by
The sweetness of our voice
We will give a blessing to everyone
And the people will say
I have never felt so good
In the theater

Get your mask
Hold it up
Lower your voice
Maiden master monster
Lover All here All there

And we will believe
And we all will say

I have never felt so wonderful after seeing a play

And we will hug Jere

And all will be well
On Mill Mountain
That night

First, you have to run the water. I like mine on the hot side. Some people take warm baths but I think "no": if it's a bath it should be hot. Now that the bathroom is steaming, light a couple of candles. They can be any scent you like. I like the woody kinds of things, personally, but lavender works and so does vanilla or peach or something but I never much cared to smell that fruity. It's just a personal thing. Then you generously sprinkle mineral salts. I know, I know. Someone will say well I like to have bubbles when I bathe but let's face it, friends. We are now grown. Bubble baths are for youngsters who think it's sooooooo funny to make a beard out of the bubbles or maybe even for young adults in love for the first or second time who are trying to be seductive and think Marilyn Monroe or someone looked sexy in the bubble bath but don't have enough sense to separate the movie from reality and who, if they are silly enough to fill the tub with bubbles, will find they must then rinse them off or itch all the way through: which we all know will not be fun. Salts. Its that simple, folks. And everything will smell great, too. Now for me it's jazz. It's a personal thing. There is something about John Coltrane's ballads or Prez's smooth sound or if I need a mood lift the swinging sound of Duke letting Johnny Hodges take a solo that . . . well . . . just makes everything all right. Ease into the tub. It's good that it's a bit too hot because the blush makes you reach for that wonderful bottle of champagne. Or, okay, let's face it . . . a blanc de blanc because champagne is too wonderful and too expensive to drink alone so the cheap stuff, a nice blanc de blanc, is just fine. Jazz. Candles. The evening is already looking up.

It's 11:30 P.M. and you are feeling quite warm and comfortable in your tub. The main advantage about being over thirty is you no longer have to pretend you have a date on Friday night or even, lo and behold, that you want one. You can now easily say to yourself, "I hope no one wants to ask me to do anything because I am so looking forward to a hot tub and a midnight snack." Do Not Answer The Phone. There will be someone on the other end whom you dislike who will insist that you come to so and so's party and you really don't like so and so but you are forced to go because you . . . Answered The Phone! Don't! You'll be a lot happier.

Getting out of your wonderful bath, you towel off and reach for your favorite lotions. Indulging each toe, each finger, every part of your back, you lotion up. It feels wonderful. You put warm oil on your scalp. You feel renewed. Positively renewed. Your dog comes to sort of sigh to say she agrees this is a new you. You reach for that heavy, thirsty bathrobe you felt guilty about purchasing on your recent visit to L.A. Yes, it was a business trip and No you did not actually need it but you were tired and you wanted something, anything that made the stress and strain of travel seem worthwhile. A three-hundred-dollar bathrobe did the trick. Then comes the best part.

You have aired your mattress and changed your sheets. You have fluffed out your comforter. You casually walk back to your kitchen, where you open the refrigerator. There are only two important things there: scallions, which you will snip into little pieces into a beautiful finger bowl which you know is for fingers but you also know holds exactly the amount of cut scallions you will want. You splash just a bit of olive oil infused with Meyer lemon or perhaps orange essence over them and, looking over your shoulder to be sure no one else is around, you take from your hidden place in the cupboard your *Sel de Mer*. You have never loved anyone enough to share this salt but you know that the moment you do wish to share, it will be *true love* and you will live happily ever after. You pinch your thumb and first two fingers over the Sel de Mer, bringing just the right amount to the scallions. Then you go back to the refrigerator. You take out the cold fried in butter chicken wings. You put them on your most beautiful "little" plate. You decide as silly as it may seem to others to take a linen napkin. You pad, exquisitely robed, lotioned, warmed to your bed. You slide under the comforter. You reach for your DVD remote and press Play. You eat and drink your heart out while you watch Michael Corleone rule the world. Can it get any better? you ask. No. This is the best midnight snack ever. And if you fall asleep on the movie . . . well . . . you own the entire collection . . . you can finish watching when you awake and have your decaffeinated Blue Mountain coffee (which you don't have to share, either).

POETIC CHICKEN WINGS

½ stick butter (salted or unsalted)
2 cloves garlic
A bit of rosemary
1 package chicken wings (with any luck Amish or at least free range)
Mrs. Dash seasoning
⅓ cup flour (approximately)
1 medium yellow or white onion

Place butter, garlic, and rosemary in electric skillet. Set skillet to about 250°F. Rinse chicken wings and pat dry. I put two or three paper towels in my sink and, tucking the tip under the drum, place the wings on them. Sprinkle Mrs. Dash on the wings. The average package has about six to eight wings. Be generous but not crazy. Lightly sprinkle the flour on the wings. Always keep an eye on the skillet. The butter, garlic, and rosemary should be melted and sort of sizzling. Place the wings in the skillet. Slice the onion as thin as is prudent. Not invisible but not thick. Add the onions to the skillet. Go do e-mail or snail mail. In about 20 minutes come back to the kitchen to turn the wings. Some of the onions will be very brown. Treat yourself to them now. Don't wait. If you like your

wings crisp, just let them finish cooking through;
if you like them a bit softer, put the top on your skillet.
While you are waiting these last few minutes, make
pepper.

HOUSE MADE POETIC PEPPERCORNS

1 saltcellar
Peppercorns
Allspice
Ground cloves
Nutmeg
Paprika

Using your pepper grinder, grind a good "bottom" of
pepper into the salt cellar. Add allspice, cloves, nut-
meg, and paprika to the fresh-ground pepper bed.
Mix to the eye. It should be attractive. This is an art
and will change every time you try it. It is excellent
for "dipping." Dinner's on.

But wait! Don't throw away those wings you didn't eat.
Save them for the best ever midnight snack!

Good & Plenty was a really dumb sort of candy with ugly ugly colors that was sold in the movie houses . . . I liked the popcorn because it was warm and a nickel and the butter was real but I grew up in a small southern town where the popcorn person probably went out back and milked the cow for butter though I guess it's only fair to say the corn was stolen from the Indians and if we had been forward looking in the old days of segregation we would have baked a sweet potato which we could have sold for pennies and started some sort of a trend

Good and plenty was Sunday dinner which was actually cooked on Saturday because Sunday church took up a lot of time and if grandmother had had to cook when she came home we probably wouldn't have gotten to eat until it was time to go back for the evening program though grandpapa never churned the ice cream until after church and the rolls were never ever put into the oven until we came in from morning services and I didn't or couldn't eat until I delivered the plates to the sick and shut in and I gotta say that was not a hard thing to do because everybody was always so glad to see you

Good and plenty is a cornucopia which is actually some sort of saxophone and I'm a big John Coltrane fan but I also love Prez who hoisted his sax on the side and blew the bluest blues so that was always a question whether or not Parker had a horn of plenty or just blew plenty horn

And somewhere out in that netherland of race and politics and growing up and growing old there is still this horn that sits in my head and though I don't have the energy to push any notes through I also am not crazy enough to say its fruits aren't edible and I sometimes sit with the moonlight dancing in my quilted lap and listen to the universe of the *midnight sun* 'cause whatever a horn is it's just got to have those Hampton vibes to make all wishes come true

THE LEAVES

The leaves in fall
are the colors
of the rainbow
Like the faces of all
people
Like the fishes
in the waters
Like the chipmunk
when the cat is near
scurrying to the shadows
hiding in the darkness
burning warmth
at the evening
and a crispness
in the air
remains as they
ascend

SANITY (TO BE CONTINUED)

FOR PREPARING LEADERS FOR A WORLD COMMUNITY

Know the truth
>When you hear it
Know beauty
>When you see it
Understand love
>When you feel it
And as you dance
>Always dance on that floor
>Polished by the best
>Of you

If I had read "Those Winter Sundays" before Bob Hayden taught me at Fisk maybe I would have understood the "chronic angers" better

If I had explored "The Negro Speaks of Rivers" rather than jumped on over to the jazz poems I would have understood the journey better

If I had heard Nina sing Waring Cuney I would have found myself beautiful

I did know . . . as beautifully as he wrote . . . that Countee Cullen was wrong to puzzle why *God would make a poet black . . . and bid him sing*

What other color should a poet be . . . no matter what the color anyway . . . didn't Jesus love the little children . . . and didn't we all live in his hands . . . and who is Allstate anyway . . . why I've been rocked in the bosom of Abraham but that's just a southern Baptist girl looking back wishing there was a mirror instead of this

I live in a prism

No matter which way the prism turns the light strikes and makes me dance

I, too, sing but no one wants to listen

Maybe I can grab a few grapes and squeeze them for wine

Maybe not . . . no miracles here . . . just a poet trying to make sense of the senselessness

The South lost . . . and that is good . . . and that hateful flag needs to come down . . . and reparations need to be offered and if none of that can happen . . . well . . . let there be poetry

This is the urgency . . . Live! said Gwen Brooks and so we do

She could have added Love. Plus a slice or two of pizza and we have a reflection. Good for us.

FIRST DATE

(FOR HERBERT ALBRIGHT)

Do we ever remember our first real date
Or do we ever really forget it
Herbert Albright invited me
At sixteen for drinks at Babe Baker's
A local watering spot for hip folk of color
Everyone had a crush on Herbert
He was older
He was good-looking and
He was so cool
I was surprised
That Mommy let me go
(Even then I wasn't old enough to drink
Though everybody did)
And I looked cool
So I was never challenged
We walked in those days
Nobody had a car
Or if it was special
You took a cab

There was a song: *I'll be down*
To get you in a taxi honey better be ready about half past eight

And you knew not to be late because the cab would leave
And you'd have to walk way too far

Herbert came on foot
But the cab met us at my house

I looked good

Face made up heels really high and polished to a T
Black dress and pearls

He looked better
A caramel cashmere suit that was made to fit him
A shirt with French cuffs that I knew cost more than my dress
His tie tied as if he were the Duke of Windsor
Black leather shoes shining so bright you
would think they were patent leather
And a charcoal gray cashmere scarf

I countered with elbow-length baby-soft black leather gloves

Still he looked better

CC and ginger, he ordered and I knew enough to say
Bacardi and Coke
I think he was being teased about me because there was laughter
That I didn't understand

The jazz band played and I knew the music
I think I looked like I belonged though I found out later
Babe was a drinking buddy of my dad's
(who wasn't?) and knew
I was too young

Avondale was too far to walk and cabs go only one way
So we started for the bus stop

I was chilly but trying not to show it

Herbert took his charcoal gray cashmere scarf
And very gently wrapped it around my neck

I am sixty-one years old . . . I still have that scarf

HOME

The bees in the field
Are refusing to yield
Until their throats are filled
With honey

The cat in the brush
Is not in a rush
Since he actually has
No money

Now me and the bird
Won't take the cat's word
The bird and I go
On home

We have us this place
Far from the rat race
Where no deer
Nor buffalo
Roam

A LIBRARY

(FOR KELLI MARTIN)

a Library Is:

a place to be free
to be in space
to be in cave times
to be a cook
to be a crook
to be in love
to be unhappy
to be quick and smart
to be contained and cautious
to surf the rainbow
to sail the dreams
to be blue
to be jazz
to be wonderful
to be you
a place to be
yeah . . . to be

FOR SUMMER

For the sheer exuberance of
singing out loud
dancing with yourself
painting a sunset red
or at least pretending that you can

For the joy of
sowing seeds for tomorrow
hope for the future
believing in the impossible
dreaming the ridiculous

For the wonder of
clapping your hands
stamping your feet
wiggling your ears

For Summer

YOUR PILLOW

I am your pillow

When you need
To lay your head
I make room
For you I create
A space
In me
That only you can fill

Your imprint will stay
Until you fluff me
Out

When you cry I muffle
Your sound
When you are cold
I snuggle
Near
I am soft
      Cool
      Pliable
And always waiting
For you to reach
Out
And hold me
Close

I DON'T WANT TO LOVE

I don't want to love
You I want to dream
I'm in your arms
In a good hotel
In a world-class city
With the lights streaming
Through

I don't need to love
You I need to dance
A dangerous dance
Of freedom
And recklessness
My dress flowing
With the breezes
Coming gently off the shore

Love is not one
Of the possibilities
Of us We are
Too old Too tired
Too tied To true
Love

But wouldn't it be
Fun
To be young
In love
In sane
In your arms

I AM YOUR ALLERGY

I am your allergy
I tickle your nose
          And make you sneeze
I squiggle in your hair
          And you think it's dander
          You don't need to change
Shampoo
          You need to change
Lovers
I wisp on your back
          And make you hug yourself
To stop
An unstoppable
Itch

Library
St. Marys Middle School
979 South St. Marys Rd.
St. Marys, PA 15857